Renouncing Holy Logic

Exposing the Secret Codes of Control, Power, Leadership and Success

Rami Anabusi

ISBN: 9789655997675

WARNINGS TO MY READERS

❧

1. **It is within your sole responsibility** to read this book with your full attention.

    <u>**The author is not responsible for any unintentional results or side effects.**</u>

2. **It is highly recommended** to read the **Whispers about the Book**.

3. **Before you read the book, it is absolutely necessary** to read the dedication on the following page. **If you do not find yourself in the dedication, <u>this book may not be for you.</u>**

To those who possess a "dead" conscience only:

The author retains all copyrights; <u>reflect before you transgress or steal!</u>

To my caring father

Whom I challenged in all rudeness

To my beloved mother

Who struck me with shrewdness

To my dear grandfather

Whose cane I angered

To my older brother

Who saved me and whom I nearly killed

To my brilliant daughter

Who taught me a lesson

To the city of Jerusalem, which has been undermined by strife

To the gentle girl who startled me

To the neighbors and relatives who rallied around me

To the moment in which I died

To everyone who searched and scraped and dug and sought but did not find

To everyone who tried every path but never arrived

To every successful person and every failure

To every pessimist and optimist

To everyone homeless and sheltered

To everyone miserable and happy

To the repressed and oppressed of the free world

To the scoundrels of humanity and the villains

To every mother and father

To every student

To every teacher

To every struggler

To every leader and follower

To every wretch and wretched

To all residents of the world!

And to Him the Almighty

All thanks, praise, and gratitude

AN ILLOGICAL MAP

This is of the Grace of my Lord that He may try me, whether I thank (Him) or be ungrateful. And whoever thanks (Him), then surely he thanks only for his (own) self, and whoever is ungrateful, then surely my Lord is Ever-Affluent, Ever-Honorable. " **Quran 27:40**

WHISPERS ABOUT THE BOOK

These are some of the reactions from a carefully selected segment across cultural sectors, age groups, and class.

"A novelty in the world of books"; "Surprising and rebellious"; "The exact meaning of: Show, Don't Tell"; "The right book at the right time"; "Fried my brain"; "Nothing like it amongst books"; "Irresistible magic"; "Push storytelling magic"; "Turned my scales upside down"; "I really needed it"; "Interesting, comprehensive, and detailed"; "I found myself"; "It wouldn't let me sleep"; "It made me laugh, enticed me, stole me away"; "I wish I had read it before"; "Complements the present time and modernity"; "Finally a novel international book"; "Speaks to the mind and the soul"; "Does not sell illusions"; "As if it were spells that combined simplicity of language and depth of content"; "Extremely interesting life"; "A lot of personal wisdom to share"; "Carefully Organized"; "Clear Call-to-Actions"; "A very new age psych book"; "The next The Secret…"

INTRODUCTION

Life is much simpler than we imagine, and the realization of success is much easier than we picture; there is no need for wonders, over-philosophizing, and oversaturated programs.

This book will lead you with absolute simplicity to one of your deepest self, developmental, intellectual, philosophical, and real journeys, presenting social, childhood, school, university, work, economic, political, and international events and issues, in a simple and easy analysis stripped of formalities, conventionalities, reservations, and decorative scientific jargon.

It is a bewitching journey and a magical incantation of success, expelling the demons of reason and the ghosts of the impossible and negating the spells of insanity and the jinxes of failure.

People ask a lot of questions and are buffeted about by baffling philosophical answers, sometimes unconvincing or impractical, such as:

- Is it possible to take control of your life and reverse it or direct it toward the direction you have always dreamed? Does life toy with us or teach us? Are our varied conditions inevitable fate from which there is no escape?

- Why do we read tens of self-development books and endure consultations which sell us the latest strategies, but only turn us into glib people who are more skillful at philosophizing reality and justifying it, remaining in our same state?

- How do I escape both scientifically and practically from the gravitational force of failure which stalks my occupational, domestic, and social life?

- How do I discover myself and crack my personal cipher? How do I choose and forge the path of my future? How do I get rid of my fears and apprehensions? How do I free myself from the captivity of the dull habit and routine of my life?

You will find the answers distributed bit by bit over four acts.

The essence of the magic of this book is in its realism, as its true events take place in a complexly structured country. It does not feature a superhero, nor the possessor of a giant fortune who looks at you from above the clouds, nor a TV star who admonishes you from afar without seeing you…

Because I live your reality and the reality of the people; I speak to you from here, not from above, but from amongst the masses and in the middle of the crowd; I have taken off my necktie and come to guide you and take your hand, to walk with you step by step, to abbreviate the path for you and warn you of the obstacles.

All you need is the courage to embark on an adventure to discover yourself, to search for the innocent child lost inside of you, and to rescue the young genius whom the blows of life buried and the armies of teachers, parents, colleagues, and admonishers silenced.

And without further delay, let us begin.

The author

Rami Anabusi

ACT

I

YOU ARE THE KING

The day I miraculously survived the
explosion of an Israeli bus (August 21st,
1995)

On the morning of 21st August of the year 1995, I was on my way to the Hebrew University in Jerusalem, on board a bus owned by the Israeli company Egged. By 7:57 AM, the bus which was also boarded by a Palestinian equipped with a bomb made by Yahya Ayyash, "the Engineer," had just exploded.

The events of your life are practical lessons, instructional courses of the highest levels, tailored exactly for you with

11

precision and skill. All the events that I will relate are real. I am not Rambo, nor am I a creator of Hollywood illusions. I do not embellish with words to bewitch and entice. Consider how many fictional books and cinematic works, of which millions of copies have been published with an audience of millions, sell colorful dreams and illusions. Promising quick wealth, inner peace, marital happiness and domestic bliss, job security, or emotional stability.

Let me share a surprising secret: foreign philosophies will not help you.

Don't get me wrong. The problem is not in these innovations, as no one in their right mind would discount the value of these works. Nonetheless, we read, learn, follow, research, watch, attend workshops and seminars, and spend money without any tangible benefit. What is the secret behind this failure?

This book is different.

The events in this book are singular to me, and although they happened to me personally, this is not a biography.

It contains examples and lessons that could save you forty years of life experiences, but it is not a self-help book.

It touches on economics, trade and business, but it is not an economics book.

It touches on education, politics, society, and psychology, but it is not a book of either.

It would be a delusion to think that you will suddenly become better, richer, happier, or more successful simply by leisurely skimming through my book and then tossing it on a shelf.

You'll say: Of course I'll toss it on a shelf. Is it a holy book?

Let's be realistic, even our holy books we often leave to gather dust much of the time; don't we all do the same?

Here's another surprise: My book is just a bait to lure you towards the most important book in your life!

I was just like many others until I decoded the algorithm that had been puzzling me: Why have I not been able to rid myself of the burden of my reality despite my desperate efforts to change it?

I had excelled in school and then in university. I studied accounting and economics, and I obtained a professional license to practice as a certified public accountant. I lectured in multiple venues and went to expensive seminars. I travelled, stayed current, read, authored, discussed, and consulted. But that algorithm remained encrypted, continuing to separate my knowledge from the life to which I aspired.

This nearly drove me crazy. I needed to crack it in order to overcome that intangible barrier.

The codes were within my reach, beckoning and calling me wherever I looked, but I couldn't see them. I traveled from my hometown of Baqa to Jerusalem and then to Tel Aviv, Haifa, and Nazareth. I spent years pursuing marketing hypes and advertising embellishments. I searched at home and abroad, but I did not search in my own hand; I hadn't noticed the free lessons along my path begging me for even the slightest acknowledgement.

How many times do we search for things we lost to the point where we lose our touch with reality, only to have your child point out what was staring you in the face the entire time.

What was the cause for such blindness?

There is no single answer in life.

This was the first lesson that I was forced to reckon with after finishing school, where I had spent years learning that only one correct answer existed, and the rest are false.

I recall one of the most interesting courses in university was "Criminal Justice." It taught me, for the first time, that possibilities might not be limited, and that a criminal charge can't be stuck to someone based on speculation or a seemingly logical narrative; rather, it must be supported by concrete evidence and explanations that cannot be ambiguous or open for interpretation amongst all the possible choices. It taught me that impulsivity could mean the execution or lifelong imprisonment of a person who had not committed any offense.

A Strenuous Exam

The lecturer had an open-book exam policy. The exams were multiple-choice, which might seem easy, except for the fact that the choices were bewildering to someone who had neither understood the material in great depth, nor had practiced their Criminal Justice knowledge while investigating the choices. Several bright students failed the course and were expelled from university or delayed a year until they could retake and pass the course.

Some of the answers would go like this:

a) All responses are incorrect

b) Only the third response is correct

c) The first and second responses are incorrect

d) The first part of the fourth response and the second part of the sixth response are incorrect

All the answers were the type that made you feel as if hot sweat was streaming down your torso. I left my chair sweaty upon exiting the examination room. I would end up earning a grade of 94%, but the course was no joke.

A Hard Life Is a Training Method to Broaden Your Horizons.

You might say, "All right, here you are going back to the one answer logic, because there's only one correct answer to the lecturer's question."

I used to be like most people, with a one-sided perspective, an absolutist in my relationships, discussions, and different life aspects. But if you were to pause and take a look from a different perspective, you will find yourself seeing things differently.

You cannot simply jump to final conclusions just because a certain idea occurred to you or a certain logic appealed to you, or just because you caught your child, your spouse, or your colleague red-handed in a disgraceful situation. Similarly, you cannot sign a trade deal simply because you drool over it nor refuse it because of a gut feeling.

There Aren't Only 4 Directions

Search for choices outside the four directions. If you don't find your need within the four directions – North, South, East, and West – as the geography teacher taught you in school, then know that more directions exist: upwards and downwards, the middle and the in-between, and what's inside and around of them, because we live in an empty void without end; we do not live on a flat surface with singular sides and sharp corners!

I Struck His Honor the Judge a Blow.

Paradoxically, even the Criminal Justice lecturer also blundered. My grade was 88% before the appeal, and even though I was only a student in the department of Economics and Accounting, I had immersed myself in the subject and fallen in love with it, which granted me the courage to strike the reputable lecturer an unforgettable blow. In addition to being a lecturer he was also a judge, or so we were told, and even though the exam was multiple-choice, I had been careful to note my justifications on the back of the exam paper as a precaution.

"I circled the sixth answer - all responses are incorrect. I deserve six more points," I objected indignantly.

"Don't be so confident, and there is no need for anger. Your answer is wrong because the correct answer is number one," he said in a disdainful tone.

"But Your Honor, answer number one is incorrect because it does not take into consideration the possibility, however improbable, which occurs in this clause of the criminal penal law. It seems like this choice slipped your mind when you wrote the questions."

"And how would I have known such a brilliant possibility would occur to you? No one has ever taken notice of it over the course of years of my teaching career." He waved his hand in the air, clearly doubtful and displeased.

"Flip the answer sheet. You will see that I noted this possibility with sufficient explanation, clarifying why the first answer would have appeared correct if not for the aforementioned legal clause," I answered confidently.

"You are speaking in a highly provocative manner." He looked askance at me as he flipped the page angrily.

"No need to take points off the other students. Just give me six points and let me leave." I left him boiling mad while I was flushed with the euphoria of victory.

The Logic of I'm the Best

That was an unpleasant lesson for His Honor, the lecturer, in front of his students at the university. No matter how specialized you are in a field, do not assume that you are infallible. Remain humble, evaluate the available choices, and entertain the thought that some choices have not occurred to you. Do not rely on the choices that have become the norm in society, perhaps there is a detail no one else has noticed, and one minute detail could be the opportunity of a lifetime.

God Could Hide His Secrets in The Weakest of His Creation

Listen to your son as a father, pay attention to your daughter as a mother, consult your life partner, do not ignore your students as a teacher, do not ridicule your employee as a manager, search between the lines and behind the fence. Do not stop digging and drilling even if everyone tells you, "It's impossible, there's no benefit to be had, and someone smarter would have done it before."

The Logic of I'm The Lesser

- **How many projects have you not attempted** just because one of the larger corporations has not tried it?

- **And how many ideas have you buried** because you were afraid of criticism and sarcastic reactions?

- **And how much effort have you wasted on complicated solutions**, because a simpler alternative never occurred to anyone?

- **How many times have you reached a dead end and given up**, even though a lifeline was dangling on the roadblock blocking your path?

- **How many times have you been offered a new job opportunity better suited to your capabilities**, full of challenges and with a sizable income, but you turned it down for fear of change?

- **How many times have you planned for a wise and calculated step**, but failed to follow through at the last moment because someone else discouraged you?

Your Life Situations Are the Most Eloquent Practical Lessons

All the events we experience are mostly free, practical lessons. While some of them are exorbitant in cost, almost costing us our life, others deplete our financial or mental reserves. Most of us go from one moment to another as though the audience in a film. Even though the events concern us personally and are happening to us, we simply pass through them. You might resort to hiring expensive consultants and attending prestigious self-help seminars, based on logical theories tested on a wide swath of people, but they have not been tested on you. How can someone benefit from general theories, when they did not benefit from their own practical experiences? Nor from their personal reality, all the while they are drowning in daydreams.

They irrationally continue to walk the same path that leads them to the same fate!

My Brilliant Daughter Teaches Me a Lesson

I learned a curious lesson from my daughter Bara'a (literally "innocence") while we conversed one affable night. I began to challenge her with riddles I had learned as a child, teasing her when a riddle stumped her. "What eats but never feels full and dies if it drinks?", "What eats without teeth and does not swallow?" My child enjoyed the challenge, and she started to invent her own made-up riddles.

"What is the thing that drinks... doesn't eat... it's human... starts with the letter B?" She laid out the riddle slowly, inventing it out loud, spinning it to me bit by bit.

"This isn't a riddle," I laughed. "You say it starts with the letter B, that it doesn't eat even though it's human. This is impossible. A riddle must be logical and reasonable, it is not just putting words together."

"Daddy, I asked you a riddle and you have to answer." Bara'a laughed innocently.

"Again, there's no such thing," I said with the firmness of a confident man.

"A baby!" she cried, chortling. "A small baby! Drinks milk, doesn't eat, it's human, and it starts with a B."

I was dumbstruck for a moment, and then dissolved into laughter. **A small child taught me a lesson – do not be hasty, do not be contemptuous, do not be dismissive, do not to be haughty. She taught me to listen well, consider all the choices, and not insist as though I had all the answers.**

And now, let me try to provoke you with some economic perspectives you had not encountered in such asperous candidness.

Economics Makes You Appear Worthless

They say that an excellent advertisement is part of the process of marketing our thoughts, principles, and selves. Economists claim that our social lives and personal relationships are all based solely on economic motivations. That kind people are actually greedy merchants merely playing a character. We unconsciously engage in trade, advertisement, and marketing all our entire lives. We market both our noble and malicious thoughts, we advertise our brave and cowardly stances to our children, relatives, and colleagues. We trade in religion and morals; even ourselves we trade in the job market when we rent ourselves to whoever pays the most for our work. Whatever your goals may be, in the view of economists, you are only a greedy merchant; you sell to profit and give to take!

Ah, How Greedy and Selfish You Are

Humans engage in the process of buying and selling continuously, so that they can obtain a financial, psychological, or social benefit as it is understood within the conventions of economics. You give to the poor because you dream of heaven, because you believe that a good deed is never wasted, or because giving makes you feel good about yourself. As such, you are guilty of greed in this respect. You think selfishly, no matter how principled your motivations are, because your actions are driven by personal gain.

Remember the term "benefit," as it has a firm relationship with the cipher which moves us. Shortly, we will need this term in all its ugliness!

Are Economists Ethicists or Not?

There are no moral or amoral aspects in economics. Concepts are understood from the position of benefits and losses, services and commodities. Drugs are a commodity; they have sellers and buyers. Prostitution is a service; it has vendors and clients. This is the language that they excel in, whose arts they are proficient in. You cannot converse with an economist in any other language, no matter how hurtful or amoral that may be in your view. To them, you are a weight of mass, a compilation of interests who seeks to protect those personal interests.

Economists Lie Even If They Tell the Truth

Economists cannot simply plot you graphically, on axes of supply and demand, without generating a mathematical equation to represent you. This is what makes economics capricious, boring, hurtful, and inaccurate. They say that if you ask ten economists a single question, more than likely you will get 10 incorrect answers! If economists were honest, they would be the richest people on the planet.

A New Confession

I won't deny that I learned the arts of trade and the skills of marketing. This book is just a lure, an ad that promotes another book which is going to be authored by none other than you, and will be the most important book you will read in your entire life!

Have you heard before of the baiting strategy of marketing? The idea is simply to attract the customer to your door.

Take a moment to contemplate the social applications of this idea.

In all strands of life, you alternate between being the fisherman, the bait, and sometimes the prey. Who among us does not switch between these roles when they speak with their daughter, when their son imitates them, when their spouse disagrees with them, when they apply to a job, when they scribble on their blog, or when they are captivated by a commercial?

Advertising is part of the process of successfully marketing ourselves, our writings, our positions, and our relationships.

But the bait that attracts the target audience without them purchasing your merchandise will be another loss debited to the account of your time and money. Sometimes, the bait tempts the customer to approach the net of sales, smell the aromas, maybe even sample a taste, but it may not be enough to get them to get hooked. Your loss of a customer or target will be debilitating, because a dissatisfied customer or a hurt target will publicize their displeasure and broadcast their warnings to tens of potential targets. Meanwhile, a satisfied customer would usually not publicize the fact to anyone, or to a limited number of other people at best.

A scandal has a fast-spreading, malignant odor. Should you try to commit a disgraceful folly, eyes and rumors will shadow you wherever you go, and you will become the center of attention, as though a famous celebrity.

You may be wondering to yourself "For God's sake, is the author callously ignoring our humanity?"

I'm not ignoring it. I don't paint a picture from a certain paradigm, neither spiritual, material, religious, nor philosophical. Sorry, our planet is not an ideal utopia. I'm simply stripping down life for you, baring it of decorations, makeup, and masks so that you won't be surprised by contradictory and clashing human behaviors. So that you don't remain a laughingstock, a punching bag, and a doll for entertainment!

The Skill of Social Marketing

Those who are successful in a field are ordinary people, but they have overcome the fear of leadership and taking risks. They also have excelled in marketing.

- **Your beloved daughter** may not be the most loving and devoted of your children, but she skillfully marketed herself to her parents as the most careful of her siblings.

- **Your humble employee** might be the hardest-working and smartest worker, but he might not be proficient in sweet-talk, yet he does not embroil himself in competition with others.

These are simple examples of marketing successes and failures, whose source is cowardice, ignorance, the loss of marketing skills, **or indifference…**

I Was Scarred As A Result Of Indifference in 1994

After I graduated from school in 1994, I worked as a cleaner at the Blue Bay Hotel on the shore of the city of Netanya. I was just as diligent a cleaner as I had been a student. While my coworker would play and do nothing all day, I did all the work alone. When the shift supervisor would come, my coworker would mock me, falsely telling her that I don't do anything all day. I met his jokes with cold indifference, until one day I had enough and we had a shouting match, when coincidentally the supervisor was passing by. I complained to her about his slacking and indolence in completing our shared duties.

What A Jarring Shock

To my surprise, she did not believe me and began to berate me for my constant and continuous shortcomings. She then threatened to fire me, which indeed came to be a few days later after a similar incident.

I strove to defend myself, trying to prove my innocence and dedication until I wept bitter tears. Neither the supervisor, nor the hotel manager believed me at that time. **I paid dearly the price of indifference. It was not leaving my job that crushed me, but rather the injustice I had wrought on myself as a result of my indifference at the beginning. It was a practical lesson the bitterness of which I will never forget.**

Prepare to Discover Your Worlds from Surprising Angles

From now on, prepare to discover the worlds of business, economics, politics, education, society, ethics, crime, religion, and heresy.

I have entered my fourth decade after undergoing professional and life experiences, during which I have been a student, a lecturer, an accountant, an economist, a consultant, and a businessman, as well as a father, a son, a political and social activist, and a writer.

You're At the Top of My Wanted List

That's right, you're the one I'm looking for.

- Whether you are a student in grade school or university, a sports player, a laboring worker, a suffering employee, a successful businessman, an ailing adventurer, a slogging father, a resplendent wife, or a despondent educator.

- Whether you are a fugitive along the border fence, immigrating with your family on a dingy boat swaying in the middle of the ocean to the unknown!

- Whether you are a vagrant, addict, or a drunkard on the margins of life!

- Whether you are a chief of state, great person amongst your people, head of a gang, or the most wretched in the demon kingdom!

Whichever of these you might be, you are human. And even if you were:

- stripped of morals,

- devoid of conscience,

- powerless,

- void of courage,

- robbed of dignity,

- dehumanized,

- captive of your wild reasoning in the trades market,

- or slave to your desires in the prostitution market!

Don't worry, you're fine, so long as you still haven't lost your mind. Your mind is the most important factor. The thing that sets you apart is that mind, and it is the only thing that will pull you up from or lead you toward wealth or poverty, happiness or wretchedness, loftiness, or decline.

I Place It in Your Hands

I present you distillations, glimmers, tools, and life experiences in an effort to formulate the most complicated of them with a simple eloquence that can be easily consumed and digested.

My Mission: Read Your Personal Book

My mission is for you to be able, after reading my book, to open your own personal book, your book which you have neglected for years and left to gather dust. The most important book from which you can learn. You are its author and its protagonist. Your life's book, which you live every day and which drives you to where you do and don't know, unconsciously surrendering to your fate. Your book which continues to apply to you failed and successful experiences so that you can learn, and practices on you gentle and tough lessons so you can wake up, not so you will be hurt.

You Are the Most Beautiful Story in The World

Believe me, you are the bravest, the most beautiful, and the most loyal. All you need is to have the courage to embark on an exciting adventure to discover yourself, to search for the innocent child lost inside of you, and to rescue the young genius whom the blows of life buried, whom the rebukes of teachers, parents, colleagues, and admonishers silenced. They wanted you lesser and lost.

Your Life Is Endless Beginnings.

Your whole life is prefaces without endings. Every situation is a preface to a subsequent prologue, and a result of a previous preface. There are no endings, but only beginnings. No matter how boisterous, miserable, or iridescent the events of your book are, your life is all beginnings until you take your last breath. The moral is to make each event be the beginning of something better. Don't you dare believe in the theory of endings and conspiracies and preordained fate. **Even death is the introduction to a new beginning and another life!**

Get up and start over again. Do not be afraid of new beginnings, because they will certainly lead you to other new beginnings and paths.

And The Bus Was Blown Up by A Palestinian Suicide Bomber in The Face of My Naivety

I had started to tell you about my first visit to the Hebrew University, on the 21st of August 1995. It was

Orientation Day for freshmen, so that they are familiarized with the university's facilities and rules, and to register in the different programs and courses.

The Excitement of Ignorance

I was excited as I boarded the bus for the first time in my life to visit my to-be university. My feelings were a mixture of fear and anticipation. I had no acquaintances to put me at ease.

My Caring Father

My father took me in his car before sunrise from Baqa to the bus station, in the city of Hadera. I anxiously boarded the bus, feeling my way like a strange cat sniffing an unfamiliar place. Most of the passengers on the bus were soldiers on their way to the barracks. I slowly took my seat, stealing a glance at the driver, only to see him scrutinizing me with intense, apprehensive flashes whose meaning I did not understand.

And the Bus Took Off

The bus took off, speeding toward Tel Aviv, where I took another bus to Jerusalem. I reached the station and ran quickly toward a bus to Mount Scopus (known as *Jabal al-Masharif* in Arabic and *Har HaTsofim* in Hebrew).

A Funeral at Home

My mother was at home with my younger siblings, enjoying the happiest moments of the summer holidays, when my father, uncharacteristically, returned home early from work.

My father showed signs of dread and confusion. My mother was shocked by the news that my father whispered to her, and the caravans of relatives and acquaintances began to arrive at our house while the children played. Everyone was speechless, huddled around a radio relating the details of the explosion of Bus 26 carrying students to their university and soldiers to their barracks. The news indicated five people were killed and dozens wounded, while live interviews were being conducted with the wounded, frightened, survivors, analysts, and scaremongers.

My aggrieved father lost his mind as he waited by the phone for it to ring, so he could reassure himself about the safety of his son who was missing amongst the crowd. He waited, everyone waited, for the ring to disperse their fear and tear into the silence. **Oh, how difficult it is for the train of life to fall silent in the middle of the road a moment before happiness!**

My father could not bear the helpless silence, he would have left for Jerusalem to search for his beloved son had my brother-in-law not dissuaded him from the idea and convinced him that the roads were cordoned off by security. They began calling the emergency lines, who told them that my name was not included on the list of wounded, and that I might be amongst the death count. Those giving solace, those giving condolences, and curious onlookers arrived successively to our house. What an unlucky day was my first day at university, and perhaps it would have been my last!

My Speeding Towards the Bomb.

I had disembarked in the central station in Jerusalem. I struggled to find my way toward the exit, stumbling in the alleys, asking passersby for directions. Time was quickly running out, and I began to run panting toward the bus. ut Unfortunately, the bus had left without me, and now I would certainly be late!

I waited for the next bus and boarded it. It moved inchmeal, maneuvering between the traffic. . The looks from the passengers preyed on me for a reason I had not yet become aware of. I listened to the radio describing a bombing of a Jerusalem bus whose number I could not make out amidst the sounds of surprise.

We reached Mount Scopus, where I followed the convoys of students walking to the university campus. I passed the outer security gate and pushed towards a large hall the students called "the lobby." I looked for a payphone to call home and joined one of the shortest queues, but its slow progress forced me to give up on the idea of waiting. I still had to find the auditorium where the Opening Day Ceremony was to be held. I did not see great harm in trying again later to call home, after the commotion had calmed down.

I found the auditorium, at last. I met my first two classmates that day: Yousef and Nasr from the town Kafr Kanna. I found them in a removed spot, away from the accusatory looks. I felt a great ease with them, and later a friendship would blossom between us.

My Phone Call Home

After the meeting, I passed by a payphone and remembered to call home. I don't recall who exactly answered the call, but the conversation was calm, or so I thought. I apologized profusely, expressing my regret. I explained that I had not been able to find a payphone, and I ended the call quickly. Exhausted, I dragged myself home. Taking one bus to a second, then a third, and then a taxi, I finally I arrived home at dusk.

A Surprise Welcome

I entered the house to find the hoard overwhelm me with kisses and hugs in overjoyed welcomes; I felt as if I were a genie who had suddenly descended from the sky. I was not aware of the reason behind this exaggerated welcome, until they recounted the events from the moment they heard the news of the explosion shortly before eight in the morning, until the phone rang when I called later in the day.

That explosion did not tear my body apart, but it decimated any dream of a rosy life and shattered my childish innocence. It showed me that reality is fraught with danger, mystery, and conflicts.

The Danger of a Single Goal and Singular Path

When you draw for your child a single goal in life, you give them a single way of life, one path without an alternate route. Through the lens of academic excellence, don't be surprised when they don't take other matters with the seriousness you had wished for. My primary goal was to not miss the orientation day. So even though I had enough time to call home, the combination of terror at the news, the tense stares, a complicated political situation, and a reality I had never experienced before, my mind was focused solely on getting to where I needed to be.

An Arab as a time bomb

I had not realized until that moment that the word "Arab" was not a race, lineage, or nationality. Rather it is an accusation, one that would follow me, as if I were a time bomb. My thoughts began to race, blurring the once-clear vision of my dreams. If I wanted to live with dignity, I had to ignore the distractions that besieged me and approach reality as it was, without guilt or remorse for which I had no fault in.

Lessons And Morals Along the Way:

- **Don't regret a train you missed**, milk spilled, time past, or business opportunity forfeited; you don't know what future you were shielded from. Grief will not help you.

- **Embrace the new beginning,** ride the next wave, move forward without looking back.

- **Ignore the suspicious looks,** hold your temper. Being different means that you are unique. Don't let discrimination stop you. Your life's book has only one author – you. It only has one pen, the one in your hand. Your decisions and behaviors are the ink it is going to be written with. You are the most important reader of your book, and its greatest beneficiary.

- **Be assured, you won't die before your time.** Even if you were to knock on death's door with all your might or run at it full speed.

That Was Not the First Time

That was not the first time I miraculously escaped death. Over twelve years earlier, when I was in first grade, I received two life lessons which nearly sealed my fate. This was the only way to make me truly understand the lesson when gentle teaching methods did not work.

Life lessons are like this. They often start with simple lessons, a gentle and safe method of teaching, but if we do not benefit from these lessons and comprehend them well, then life will teach us the same lessons using a different method, which may be harsher and tougher. Despite this, these tough lessons might not help us if we do not possess the skill to solve the algorithm of the logic that controls us, binds us, and prevents us from accomplishing our goals.

Don't worry now, we will decipher it code by code shortly.

For now, I offer you a simple introduction to the algorithm of that logic, through the analysis of three life events that I experienced in my youth:

1: My First Escape from Death

School rules prohibited students from leaving the school from the West entrance. It was known as the Street of Death, due to the number of lives that dangerous street had taken. All students must enter and exit from the East side, where it was safe. The love to discover and the adrenalin of adventure constantly called to me, since kindergarten, to the Street of Death. Something drew me to take that scary road, where the cars sped down narrow lanes. The most dangerous leg of it was crossing the junction, known to this day as the Shabra Junction. I had to cross from its west side to the east side where our home was.

When you uncover a person's code, you control him!

I convinced my close friend to take the Street of Death on our way home. My friend was the leader, due to his power and size. I took advantage of his algorithm with cunning. I easily convinced him and had him wrapped around my finger. It was not in his power to refuse because he did not want to appear a coward. I was the thinner one and he was bigger.

We took that road on the way back from school, dread sweeping over us as the cars sped by, the fear and the anxiety of being discovered by the teacher or our families gnawing at us.

Our adventure reached its climax at the Shabra Junction, where our field of vision narrowed. Cars sped by, but we could barely see them. I took the chance first, after a long hesitation, crossing the junction while my heart pounded with fear. I waited for my friend on the opposite side, encouraging him until he finally crossed hurriedly. It was an indescribable rush. I could not believe I had managed it.

If a logic works again and again, that doesn't necessarily mean it's right.

We followed an incorrect logic, but it worked. If you ran at full speed, then no car would hit you, because the crossing distance, the width of the street, is short. We repeated this several times, and our only obstacle was the Shabra Junction, but the logic of running fast solved this problem for us, little by little, with each escape.

Until one day, I ran quickly and confidently to cross the junction, and a car suddenly appeared speeding south. I had not noticed it at first, but I heard the screeching of brakes in my ears, followed by a crash, and then the shattering of glass. I froze on the other side and looked back trembling.

I did not fully realize in that moment what had happened. I did not comprehend how I had caused the accident. I only understood that I was the cause of the disaster. I stayed at home replaying the images in my mind. I realized that the first car had been about to hit me, and so its driver braked abruptly, after which it was hit by a second car from behind.

I had glimpsed the shattered headlight glass. I was overwhelmed by the scene of the drivers' hysteria and the swarm of people getting a closer look at the damage. I forgot my friend and had run off to my house, not stopping for anything. My heart filled with terror.

What if my father or my teacher were to find out?

I spent the day and night worrying about the next morning.

My friend was eager to narrate the events of the previous day to everyone, illustrating for them in the tiniest details the accident I had caused the day before. He was recounting it as if telling a magical story from wonderland. At the time, we did not know police films or action games. Even though I was the hero of the story, the limelight was stolen by my friend returning from the site of battle. He was a storyteller; young boys gathered around him as he artfully recounted the frightful events, imitating the sound of the brakes and the *boom* of the impact. They have been told about the Street of Death from which children never escape numerously.

Reliance on incorrect logic makes breaking away from it difficult.

All the while, I was still thinking of returning to the Street of Death once again. The logic of running fast had proved its efficacy; I had passed between several speeding cars safe and sound. In the worst-case scenario, the cars would hit each other, and no harm would come to me.

The children were eager to listen to the story, amazed at my escape from between the claws of certain death. I had returned from the dead. I did not see anything strange in my escape, because the speed running method made my survival logical and certain.

Nevertheless, I was sad and fearful, my limbs trembling, of something else. Dire consequences awaited me now that the incident would almost certainly come to the teacher's attention. The echoes of my deed had spread to an extent impossible to contain. I sat in my seat waiting for the first period like one who waited for a death sentence for an unprecedented crime.

The teacher entered as if the Angel of Death himself, and the tattletale jumped up to tell the teacher the news of my deed. He listened to my friend's story with apparent keen. He called me to the board and questioned me in front of everyone. I denied everything and swore heavy oaths that my friend was a liar. But the tattletale stuck to his story, and began to tell details of the accident and its damage in a way that left no room for doubt.

At that time, it was not quite as easy for a child to imagine the details of an accident, the sound of the impact, the breaking glass, and the hysteria of people. His ability to relate it in distinct detail and with great zeal evidenced the truth of his testimony.

There's a way out of every predicament in life, but

I had to get out of this predicament with a convincing excuse after I had been stuck with the charge. So I shifted the blame to my friend, claiming that it was he who had coerced me into going by the Street of Death, that it was he who had, in jest, pushed me into the junction until he nearly killed me. I loudly pushed the charge away from me and cast the blame onto my friend, supporting it with all the vows I could think of.

My second story was logical, since my friend was the largest in the class and its leader, and I was the thinnest. Logic commanded that it was he who had dragged me to the highway, and it was not far-fetched that he had pushed me and nearly killed me with his joke.

The timing factor is important!

I had not had the courage in the beginning to falsely accuse my large friend, because he would have taken revenge on me, and I would have lost his friendship and protection.

I should have complained about my friend to the teacher first, and then the court's decision would have definitely been in my favor. But my denial of the accident's occurrence at the beginning of the questioning shook the teacher's confidence in my second story even though it appeared logical. The judge handed down his final judgment, as if he had been waiting on tenterhooks for the opportunity.

The lesson of timing, which I had just learned from the teacher's shaken confidence in my second story, could have saved me from my scar with indifference which led, 12 years after that moment, to my firing from the Blue Bay Hotel.

The teacher wore a silver analog watch, loose on his left wrist. I remember it as I remember him. He took it off and placed it on his desk in preparation for carrying out the sentence. As he came closer to me, I begged him to believe me. He ignored my pleas for mercy and held my cheek with one hand and slapped the other cheek with his other hand. He slapped my face several times. I don't remember how many. Each time I swore, he slapped me. If I wailed, he slapped me; whimpered, he slapped me.

That was the harshest and longest punishment I had tasted in my life.

If only he had stopped for a moment, granted me a moment to catch my breath, which was impeded by my crying. He hit me with what felt like two dozen stinging slaps, each jerking my head and shaking my neck.

His concern was the steel and the glass.

His anger and punishment were not because he feared for my life. My crime was that I caused damage to the cars. My life, that I nearly lost, didn't concern him, he didn't care about my mental state. His concern was for the steel and glass, as if it had been his car that was damaged.

I hated him.

He did not take issue with the behavior of my friend, who had broken the rules just like me. We were both children, who had committed the same transgression by taking the Street of Death. As for the accident, that was not my fault. I was a child, and of course I did not intend to cause harm. The accident was caused by the second driver, who failed to keep a safe distance. **In short, I hated that teacher with all my heart!**

They Commit Crimes They Do Not Perceive

Because of fear,

- I committed atrocities: I lied, fabricated, and swore falsely.

- I did not tell my father about the accident. I feared his punishment.

- I did not complain to my father about my teacher's crime. I suppressed my agony.

We commit a crime toward our children when we punish them unjustly, relying on fear and intimidation alone. We push them toward incorrect behaviors and delinquency, antithetical to our intentions. We stuff them full of psychological traumas and resentments that eat at their hearts.

I was lucky.

I was lucky that I had been naughty since I was little and was used to stirring up trouble and receiving punishments. I feel fear, but I am not a coward. Because of that I did not need psychological treatment after the accident, or as a result of the criminal punishment which followed it. Another student perhaps would have been permanently scarred after the two shocks. As for me, I returned to the fast street.

The wrong punishment exacerbates wrong behavior.

Hitting was never a successful way to deter me, my stubbornness and persistence only increased. The punishment that day exceeded the limit of discipline, transformed it into a vengeful crime and monstrous torture. I glimpsed in his eyes a depraved glint as he got creative with launching attacks that my weak defenses could not block. He would savagely remove my hand from my face and replace it with a resounding slap.

We come across road signs in our path. So, what meanings does the warning sign of punishment hold?

A leader understands: Go cautiously.

A coward understands: Don't try.

Many lessons in one event

Even our worst experiences have many benefits. Our entire lives are lessons, including our mistakes, and its punishments are preparation to ready us to cross roadblocks that await us. **For example:**

- **Two wrongs don't make a right, and impulsivity only makes it worse.**

I deliberately lied, accused my friend, and did not escape from punishment. Three huge losses. With a little self-restraint, I could suffer only one loss, but when we allow panic logic to control us, we leave the bounds of reason. This, in turn, makes us dig ourselves in even further. I should not have lied nor accused my friend, because that would not have altered the punishment.

- **A man's company goes bankrupt;** the logic of arrogance and fear of scandal takes over, so he drowns himself in heavy debts and overdrawn checks. He gets entangled in the underworld, mortgaging his house and his properties. He loses his company and his reputation; he loses everything he owns.

- **A child drowns in front of their parents**, so the father jumps in and the mother follows him though neither of them can swim, so an entire family drowns as a result of an impossible rescue mission.

- **Someone is angered by an aggravating situation,** or some upsetting news. They break their mobile phone in a haze of rage. Then they scramble to pick up the fragments, and search for a technician to save the lost data.

- **An angry husband** physically assaults his wife, then his children, then destroys their valuable belongings. Sins and losses that pile up on top of each other.

- **A woman is fired from her job**, so she burns the bridge with a scalding attack on the company and its owners. She loses their recommendations for a subsequent opportunity, and the door is slammed in the face of future opportunities that had been looming on the horizon.

- **Mass crimes are committed** yearly in the United States, which claim students and educators as victims without reason or mercy.

- **I discovered my friend's attachment to me.**

I accused him and no disaster happened. Indeed, we remained friends, which explains many of our incorrect analyses. We were connected by a mutually beneficial childhood relationship, each helping the other. I needed his muscles, and he needed my brains. Mutually beneficial relationships are stronger than exchanged insults.

From an unethical perspective, had I known that my friend was attached to me to such a degree, I would have taken advantage of his attachment, and I would have slandered him and taken him down before he slandered me.

We see this often in our lives:

- An employer takes advantage of his employee's financial need… **subsistence extortion.**

- A worker takes advantage of his employer's dependence… **employment extortion.**

- A young man takes advantage of a girl's sincere love for him… **emotional extortion.**

- A woman takes advantage of a man in a bind… **sexual extortion.**

When you reveal your cards or codes to someone, you become susceptible to extortion.

- **Follow the astronomical numbers in the stock market,** and for how much the stocks of technological companies, especially growing companies, are bought and sold. When the giants battle over an idea or innovation, stock values skyrocket.

- **When you buy or sell a car from a showroom,** the car dealer will ruthlessly take advantage of you as soon as he smells your need, he will most likely give you no mercy.

- **In the Iraq War of 1991,** Saddam Hussein launched Scud missiles at Israel. Panic ensued that the rockets might contain chemical warheads. People flocked to buy adhesive strips to seal windows and doors, fearing the purported gas attack, resulting in the prices for adhesive strips jumping exponentially.

- And why go far? **During the latest coronavirus pandemic,** the prices for masks rose to astronomical figures.

- **Gaining multiplied courage:**

After I was punished in front of them the first time, being punished in front of the whole class no longer worried me. And after the cruelty of the punishment, no punishment scared me. That punishment refined my personality in a way that made me brave to the point of recklessness, unafraid of any punishment. My feelings and emotions dulled; a rebellious spirit overtook me.

The multiplied courage was the best and most dangerous benefit.

This third benefit was very important so as not to lose my self-confidence in front of the students. But it was a double-edged sword; it made me reckless, paying no mind to society or people. I no longer feared anything, I no longer dreaded anyone, no punishment could scare me anymore, and I was encouraged to undertake any adventure no matter how difficult it appeared as long as it did not touch certain death. **Only the phobia of dogs and heights was I unsuccessful in overcoming.** It was impossible for me to be rid of this new complex, which was the result of flawed education, except by a tailored life experience whose consequence would be more acutely painful and leave a deeper mark.

What punishment would be harsher? Perhaps this offers an explanation into why punishments may not help some personalities, no matter how drastic the punishment is.

Where would a wise educator, who would understand my algorithm, come from?

It's life. How eloquent are its lessons and how wise its admonitions.

2: I Returned to My Fate and Nearly Died This Time

No matter how easy or difficult an experience is, it is

a life lesson for your future. But first, you must correctly understand the lesson. As for me, I had learned from my first occurrence an important lesson, which I understood from the slaps, that going to the Street of Death had to be a secret. This is a lesson that a stubborn adventurer will understand, even if he is young. When he is punished with such brutality, tortured savagely with the goal of breaking him, frightening him.

Meanwhile, my classmates learned the lesson of cowardice. No one wished to be in my place, to be displayed in front of everyone. They were subdued for a long time to come.

I returned to the Street of Death by myself, without any witnesses.

I crossed the dangerous Shabra Junction with great caution and lightning speed. I crossed to the east side safely without any bangs or brakes, my eyes glinting with the flame of challenge and the fire of vengeance.

Then I started to cross the next street, which led to my house. As I was crossing, I heard the sharp sound of brakes from an approaching car coming toward me. I don't know by what miracle I jumped to the dirt sidewalk with an instinctive response of a kangaroo. This time I saw the specter of the car, and how close it had come to crushing me. I stood riveted in place, keenly aware of my near demise. I was struck by a shock that disabled my ability to move. It was a Peugeot, driven by a man in his late forties, his eyes shaded by translucent pale gray glasses. He threw open his car door, jumped out, and ran toward me. I was sure he would launch blows, but he shook me, aghast, and asked me reproachfully, **"Are you okay? Why did you do that? What's your name, and whose son are you?"**

I stammered as I replied. I did not know if he knew who I was. He let me go and said, **"Do you want to die, son?"** And then he left in his car.

It was clear from his facial expressions that my death was imminent. His jump from the car, his tone of voice, and his eyes pointed to intense pity and emotion. His fear for me was more apparent than my fear for myself. I also could not believe that I had not died.

For The First Time I Wet My Pants with Fear

That was the first time I felt my movements disabled and my thoughts shut down. Little by little I began to take weighted steps, I could not yet run. Then I felt hot urine flowing down, without my control. I could not control myself at all. I felt strangely comforted by this, after I had nearly exploded from my storm of emotions. So I ran in fear and embarrassment all the way home.

The Death-Challenging Game

I don't remember exactly how I resolved the matter with my mother when I returned home in that state. **That day I**

realized that the Street of Death was not a fun game for children, and that challenging death was not the best idea.

The precision of life lessons cannot be matched by any film, lesson, or human development program.

Facing death, alongside that man's pity and his edifying scolding, in the midst of my astonishment that he had not punished me contrary to my expectation, was the only way to shake my state of confusion. This led me to think realistically about the reality of death, to realize the essence of my life, its value, and the seriousness of dangers which could result. That was a stinging and profoundly educational lesson. I was in dire need of a rehabilitative punishment to twist the neck of my previously crooked logic.

A hangman's rope and a kind driver, exactly what I needed.

This lesson ended my recklessness. The car's approach toward me where it nearly killed me was like a hangman's rope dropped onto my neck, or a guillotine blade falling toward my chest. No school punishment was comparable to that. The driver, with his kind words and tender emotions as he shook me reproachfully, was the best educator for such an intractable case as mine.

The Importance of Rehabilitative Punishments, Criminal and Educational

We might make light of our practical life lessons. The hero of certain real-life events might be a young

child, but the outcomes of that occurrence and its practical applications are applicable to all the facets of educational systems, including the penitentiary system.

How many times have you heard of a criminal released from prison only to fall into recidivism? It makes you wonder, what made him do that?

Compare the teacher's harsh punishment, which was a punishment for the sake of punishment, and the driver's reaction as a rehabilitative punishment. Which of the two punishments bore fruit?

The Teacher Whose Very Harsh Punishment Didn't Even Upset Me!

I still respect my fifth-grade mathematics teacher; he never hit a child. He would call the disorderly student up with vehement anger, take hold of his hand as he waved a steel ruler in the air, and make as if to strike the palm of the hand with it. He would stop suddenly and ask, "Should I hit you or will you sit quietly?" And the disorderly student would always reply "No, I'll sit quietly!" We would return to our seats laughing at this naive teacher who got angry and did not hit.

One time during the math period, he caught three of my companions and I (the four of us were the math geniuses in the class) red-handed with the answers to the Religion Education homework from one of our notebooks. The RE teacher was also the principal of the school, around whom we walked on pins and needles.

The math teacher lost his mind, worse than ever before, and he called us to the board along with the classmate from whom we were copying the homework. He grabbed a meter-long wooden ruler that the teachers used on the board. He held it from the middle, took my hand first and waved the ruler in the air as was his usual comedic habit, but without asking me his usual question. He brought the wide ruler down onto the palm of my hand with all his might and speed.

The echo of that hit cut the sound of the students' laughter. The girls covered their gaping mouths with their hands, and the boys fell into silent wide-eyed astonishment. I was just as surprised as everyone else. No one could believe that the math teacher had actually hit a student. He had never done it before even with the worst troublemakers. So how could he hit the four of us, when we had not committed any great offense?

Each of our hands received its share of two successive resounding hits. He hit me and my three classmates, who by then were crying. As for me, I was used to it as you know!

That was the first and last time the math teacher hit a student, and he said to us in a measured voice "Great, just great. You are the brightest in class, its stars. This ugly deed coming from you? What have you left for the slackers?"

That was the punishment for which I did not resent my teacher.

3: An Event That Changed My Life

My father and my teachers did not realize the secret of my rebellious personality. When you misunderstand the personality in front of you, then you will never control it, nor will you be able understand its deviant behaviors. My behaviors differed from the behaviors of my peers and siblings.

I did not take seriously the punishment of my father, grandfather, or teachers. I did not care what the students would say. I was rebellious to the point of madness. Hitting was all they knew to do, to chastise and hit. None of them knew how to handle my personality, and then they wondered why my deviant behavior was, that no amount of severe smacking could fix.

- **I would run away from my father, outside the house,** standing at a safe distance from the outer gate, and he would stand irritated at the top of the steps next to the upper door, calling me to come inside while I shook my head, eyes full of defiance. This would add to his fury, but I was sure that he could not do anything.

He would summon my older brother, who unlike me was obedient, to come bring him my head. I would threaten him with stones that I threw at him without concern for consequence, and run away from the neighborhood, not returning home until my father's anger had extinguished. I would not enter the house until I made him swear that the punishment would be lessened.

I would cleverly take advantage of algorithms. My father was after all a parent, and no matter what I did I would remain his beloved son and he would remain my adoring father. None of my siblings other than I dared to make use of the fatherhood algorithm.

Sometimes, I would also appeal to my grandmother, God rest her soul, and she would intercede with him on my behalf. My father never refused her any request.

- **I would similarly run from my grandfather, God rest his soul, as he ran after us with his cane.** I would argue with him from afar in the same way I did with my father. He could not run after me, and what would he do if he caught me? I would stand two meters away from him, and as soon as he approached angrily, I would distance myself another three meters, and so he would throw his cane at me, and I would scoop it up and run away with it. I was a rebellious child.

- **One time I ran away from home to teach my father a lesson.** I climbed the fig tree in our garden and stayed there until after dark while they searched for me for many long hours. They would call for me and I wouldn't answer, until the house was filled with relatives and neighbors. I was watching them coming and going. I climbed down before the matter got out of hand, because

I heard them throwing around the idea of calling the police. I took refuge next to a female relative of mine, and I escaped punishment thanks to the neighbors who convinced my father to thank God for my safe return.

- **I would not do my homework over the school vacations.** I spent the vacation playing and didn't complete a single lesson or assignment. I considered it a brazen interference from my teacher in a matter that concerned my rest and how I spent my vacation. I'd rather get hit and chastised over losing a moment of excitement which could not be recompensed with all the riches of the world.

- **Why should I study and pore over books instead of playing and having fun?** Enduring a punishment for minutes or an hour, no matter how harsh, is easier by far than studying long hours and losing out on exciting adventures.

- **I would defy punishment and even hated the threat of it,** because in my view punishment was an injustice against which a revolution must be called. One time, I screamed in my father's face when he wanted to punish my younger brother, and took off running with my father shouting threats after me. Another time, I snatched the belt from my father's hand as he waved it threateningly.

The mere threat of corporal punishment increased my obstinacy and insistence on doing wrong, as a form of expression, objection, and resistance.

My father was not pleased with my rebellion, but he knew my mindset, and so for the most part he would control himself. Oh, how much my father suffered.

- **I was brave and obstinate to a point close to recklessness.** I once jumped off a wall several meters high, and none of my friends dared to challenge me in this. I felt my legs sink into the ground and my knees crack under the pressure and my hip bones shake as if about to explode. I pretended that the jump was easy and hid my excruciating pains all the way back home.

- **In fifth grade, one of our friends' eldest brother dared us** while we were at their house for his birthday. He was a soccer player in the league, and he offered 5000 old Israeli shekels, close to two US dollars today, to whoever could catch his shot and preventing it from entering the goal. His kick was skillful, and he was older than us by several years.

Everyone backed away in fear of his shot. I challenged him, pounced toward his rocket-like ball and caught it, breaking my right arm in the process. Despite the severe pain, it was a convincing excuse for three weeks; I didn't have to write or complete any assignments.

Believe it or not, all these antics and I was still extremely shy.

All this time I was still a child, and it was neither common nor accepted for a child to object to and defy punishment with such rebellion. Despite my love for my father and my respect for my teachers, their punishments pushed me over the edge and made me seem obstinate and rude.

Even so, I was extremely shy. My cheeks reddened quickly, and people described me as being shy of my own shadow. Yet if a punishment or adventure loomed on the horizon, I turned into a savage. A starved cat when it smells fish. It perplexed everyone.

And Finally: A Major Event Happened That Changed the Course of My Life

It's true that I escaped from a bus explosion, from two deadly car accidents, and from a murderous wasp attack, but the major occurrence in my life happened in sixth grade. That year I earned first place at a karate kumite championship, but that was not the major event which changed the course of my life.

At the end of the first semester, before winter break, the homeroom teacher who was also the principal of our school distributed our report cards for the semester. My order in the alphabet was number 9. The principal would call each student up to the board to stand facing his seated classmates, then the principal from his desk would announce to everyone the student's grades, their average, and their class ranking.

Despite my misbehavior and carelessness toward studying, my class rank over the years fluctuated between 6 at best and 8 at worst. Cunning cheating methods had a role in this of course, and my lower ranking sorely rankled my father. He wanted me to be the first, like my older sister, and at the end of every semester an expansive chewing out awaited me.

Childish cunning

I used to take pity on my father despite this, he did not understand me. I used to drive him crazy with my tricks. One day I returned home from playing outside, when my father called to me from his bed as he was searching my school bag. I rubbed my neck while he asked me about the religion notebook. Luckily, it was completely blank since the beginning of the year, so I told him this is a second, new notebook, and I will go immediately to my bookcase and bring the first, old one, so you can reassure yourself that I am diligent in completing my homework.

I waited a few minutes for him to call me, hoping he would forget. He didn't forget, and called out to me again, so I answered that I was still looking everywhere for my notebook, but it seemed that it had been lost. My father fell silent. I don't think he was convinced by my answer, but he had no other option.

It was my turn

I stood present for judgment in front of the students, the principal announcing my grades and average, and as soon as he mentioned my rank, he asked everyone to applaud my talent. Personally, I had not been following what the principal was saying, and I had not heard my rank which I did not care about in the first place. I already knew my grades, which were no different from before; I had as usual an evaluation of "good, 80%" in two subjects and an evaluation of "very good, approximately 90%" in one subject.

My cheeks reddened, because I was sure the principal was ridiculing my grades, and that the applause was not of honor but rather of mockery.

The principal called my name and I thought he was going to punish me, instead he gifted me a blue copy of the Quran, the prize for first place. I sat down in disbelief. No one else could believe it either. I remember one female classmate called to me from my right and said incredulously, "Not bad, first place out of nowhere!"

Purely by cheating and coincidence!

I know I didn't deserve it. I had not earned better grades than previous years, and I had cheated on some of the tests because I would sit next to a diligent classmate. I would copy off him what I was not sure of. As for him, he did not copy anything off me because of his confidence that he was "cleverer" than me. I thus earned better grades than him and others, and coincidentally the grades of the seven students who were usually ahead of me dropped, so I earned the ranking purely by cheating and chance.

Was it a coincidence? It was a life lesson tailored to my size.

I returned home happy and pleased. For the first time, I carried my report card in my hand instead of in my bag. It was a different feeling from the fear that used to overwhelm me on the report cards ceremony day, which we used to call "the holiday of belts and slippers." This time it was a holiday in every meaning of the word.

My mother was overcome with happiness, and I went out to play, eagerly awaiting my father's return this holiday. He returned in the afternoon, and I hid the surprise from him. He grabbed my report card on the spot, before he could change out of the clothes he had labored in or even take off his shoes.

The castigating refrain that preceded the flying rockets began, but before he could press the launch button, I surprised him with the blue Quran. On it, the principal's dedication. My father was overjoyed, happier than I had ever seen him before. His scolding ceased immediately, and his tone changed to one of encouragement, urging me to exert more effort in improving my grades. The only thing that had changed was that I had ranked first in my class.

That night my grandparents visited us, and my father showed them my report card for the first time in my life. His pride and joy were evident, as he showed them the first-place gift. My grandfather's short moustache pricked my skin as he kissed me in congratulations, he handed me 500 new shekels, which was a huge amount at the time. I was soaring with happiness, and my father now took every occasion and visit to boast about me and have me sit next to him.

That was like an enticing dream; I enjoyed many happy days. I suddenly became the indulged son without any warning. From misbehavior, punishments, and constant worry to respect, happiness, and love. How beautiful are commendations, appreciation, and praise.

And Then, My Life Was Overturned

I was greatly affected by the reactions of my father, grandfather, and teachers. It was a new and different feeling. I resolved to sustain this accomplishment, and therefore the love, appreciation, and safety.

My life was turned head over heels in the second semester. I stayed up long hours completing all my homework assignments, and I worked so hard that I was cut off from the adventures and friendship of the hooligans of childhood.

For the first time based on merit and worthiness, my efforts bore fruit, and eventually, I earned full marks in the second semester and ranked first place again.

One of the keys of my childhood was challenge, so punishment was the exact opposite way to turn that specific key. Life was the first educator that uncovered my algorithm. That occurrence was the perfect practical lesson that upended my life and transformed the energy of obstinacy and defiance into a stubborn determination and academic excellence.

Challenging The University Lecturer

This raging spirit accompanied me throughout my university studies. In my second year, the top students in the Economics department were invited and two textbooks were distributed to each of us as an encouraging gift. We were enrolled in a special course for top students. In the first meeting, the lecturer informed us that in groups of two or three, we would have to translate and present a complicated economics article that he gave us. Each week, a group would give their presentation in front of the class for discussion.

This was an extremely difficult challenge - translation, analysis, presentation, and discussion in front of philosophizing students and a mean lecturer whose only concern was to trip up students. He never let a student complete a thought or sentence without stopping them, embarrassing them with questions that shook their confidence, so the student would get nervous and stutter throughout the rest of the presentation. All the students hated his method.

There was a Christian student from Shefa-'Amr, who was the only Arab classmate in the course. I worked hard to convince him not to drop it, but he insisted. All my attempts to convince him did not work. He would not see himself as a laughingstock for the lecturer to toy with in front of the students, when he had seen the smartest among us with his brow beading with sweat as he stuttered and forgot the rest of his presentation. I alone remained steadfast. This increased my willpower and determination to challenge this lecturer.

Racial and ethnic discrimination were not absent from the situation. Withdrawing was impossible for me. The issue had become personal as well as nationalist.

I was partnered with a male and female classmate. I chose the first third of the article. I translated it from English to Arabic, and I prepared for it with such preparation that my cells absorbed the topic of the article and I memorized it by heart. I readied the presentation slides with care.

The Poor Calm Arab

The students were looking forward to my presentation, eager to hear a student who was very quiet during lectures. They wondered what my presence would be like in front of the other students. The signs of pity were apparent on their faces, for a certain fate awaited me at the hands of the lecturer.

That was one of the hardest challenges I have ever gone through.

The promised day arrived… I dodged his stones and gave him a rock that silenced him!

I stood in front of the students and began to present with fluency and an expressive tone as if I were an actor on a stage. Everyone's expressions turned to tremendous astonishment, listening and smiling in disbelief at what was happening. *Is this really him?*

Suddenly, the lecturer threw a stone in my path. The students' chagrin at his way of interrupting the chain of narration and train of thought by casting provocative questions as usual was apparent. I dodged his stones and lobbed a rock that silenced him.

"If you had waited a little bit, you would have found out the answer. Follow along with me."

The students cheered for my opposing stone. He did not wait long before jumping up with an even larger stone, to which I replied,

"That is exactly what I'm going to talk about now."

He went crazy, and he cast a giant rock near the end of my section, so I simply said,

"If you had paid attention to the beginning of the presentation, you would have known the answer. But don't worry, I will explain it to you again."

The students' laughter rose in spiteful cheers against a lecturer who had made a laughingstock out of all of them.

Here is an oppressed, quiet Arab wiping the floor with him in front of everyone's eyes.

Life Prepares You for Opportunities

Life was preparing me for this moment, this was not my first experience in front of an audience, I had gotten used to performing and reciting the Quran at the opening ceremonies of school events, and I participated in karate championships and scientific competitions in front of large audiences. Since sixth grade I used to ask the Arabic language teacher if I could teach the students the grammar lesson myself.

A Very Embarrassing Night

Not all my experiences were successful. One time when I was in sixth grade, I faltered at the beginning of the event while reciting the verses of fasting in front of a large assembly of principals, teachers, parents, officials, and the Chief Justice.

That same night, I missed the answers to a competition's questions in front of the audience. I was my school's representative. That caused me great embarrassment in front of my father, principal, teachers, and classmates who had been rooting for me. I had participated in another competition in which I had greatly excelled. I was the king of the event; I recited and performed as if I were The Dark-Skinned Nightingale, an Egyptian singer.

But this was a truly embarrassing night contrary to expectations.

What is important is to be ready for the next round, take the moral and move on.

Our experiences refine us. Failure should not stop you; it's okay to fall, because you only ever fall onto a moral that saves you from destruction. **It is the nature of failure to make you feel upset, because failure uses your fall to cast onto your chest the rock of despair. All you have to do is twitch for the rock to get off you. Get out of the hole you fell into and take from it the moral you fell onto; don't you dare pick up the heavy rock of despair with it, and go on lightly, accompanied by the moral that saved you and will save you from future seasonal falls.**

What is important is to be ready for the next opportunity before it comes to you, for it is better to be ready for an opportunity that doesn't come than for an opportunity to come when you are not ready.

The Title of "King" ("Melech")!

After the presentation, everyone pounced on me in congratulations and gave me the title of "King" or "Melech" in Hebrew, and the details of the theatrical presentation spread to all the students, after which everyone started to congratulate me as if I were a superhero.

Is it really possible to control your life and flip it, or direct it, toward the direction you have always dreamed of? Does life toy with us or teach us? Are our domestic, societal, and financial conditions a predestined fate from which there is no flight or escape? Are we predestined or given choice? Is it possible for us to control others' destiny and determine their behaviors?

You Are the King.

I will not reveal all my adventures at once. These were simplified introductions, but before you set off with me toward the reasoning of madmen, you must forget what you used to know, **and know from this moment onward, that in this world you are the king. Your fate is in your hands**.

Are you ready for an adventure you will never forget your whole life?

Prepare yourself to wade into the mysterious world of algorithms in the next act.

A magical incantation awaits you. One that will negate the jinxes of failure and the spells of insanity, and expel the ghosts of the impossible and the demons of logic.

ACT

ILLOGICAL CIPHERS

How and why do we read tens of self-development books and attend conferences that sell us the "strongest" management and financial strategies, but these only turn us into people who are more skillful in philosophizing reality and justifying it?

The topic of this act is grave!

Because it turns your head inside out and shakes the scales of reason which have bewitched you all your life with their spells and controlled the proceedings of your life without you realizing or resisting. You might suffer a headache from the shock of uncertainty, but with some patience and a lot of courage you will be cured of the insanity that you used to believe was the height of sense and reason.

But You're a Fierce Disbeliever?

Don't worry…so am I.

- **I'm a fierce disbeliever** in the theory of depressing conspiracies.

- **I'm a fierce disbeliever in the inevitability of fate.**

- **I'm a fierce disbeliever in assumptions that rule our world.**

- **I'm a fierce disbeliever in any human religion** interpreted according to someone's whim and fancy.

Heresy is my road to the truth, and my path to certainty, and my door toward freedom.

I'm a raging heretic…

- **I'm brave in confrontations and struggles**, even if against the greatest genius demotivators and the most eminent of them in degree and position.

- **I don't idolize theories**, and none of them appeal to me except those that can be applied, and which embolden me and grant me confidence.

- **And I choose the tools** that help to bury alive the impossible and change my reality!

Be certain...

That you will remain in ignorance as long as you live if you fear heresy and never leave the religion of the familiar; you must become a heretic my way, or else you will never be able to keep up with me, and you will never budge from your place.

I comprehended it practically only after 40; it abbreviates years from your long path and explains many of life's contradictions and illogical laws!

The Astonishing Logic: A War for Control

This astonishing logic is a double-edged sword. If you decipher its codes then nothing at all will stand in front of you; it is the grave secret that is constantly pursued by the most powerful minds in intelligence, war, politics, economics, and sociology.

Your logical codes being deciphered in a certain area will have only one meaning: your loss has certainly become imminent like an easy meal, because your playing strategy in life has been uncovered, your movements expected.

Most people have unencrypted or all-zero logical codes, which makes them easy to read and susceptible to extortion shrewdly practiced by merchants who draw you in for their economic benefits, and ideology hawkers who guide you toward their political benefits.

A Blazing World War of Minds

When a fugitive or target has an uncovered cipher, it is possible for intelligence services to lure him in to arrest or eliminate him, and for war generals to lure him in to win the opposing battle they are waging against his army. It is a blazing world war of minds for the purpose of uncovering the codes of the logic that moves others, which makes them pitiable victims. Whoever has the codes controls the string of events, rendering them predictable moment by moment, in order to direct the targets on a puppet stage toward a plot which they presume to be its heroes.

There are many who are interested in breaching your personal ciphers so they can exploit you with the ugliest or best means to achieve their goals and serve their benefits, whether you're aware or not. It's not only war generals, intelligence officers and politicians who are interested in this - it could be your boss at work or your employee, and your partner in trade or your competitor in the market, and it could be your faraway enemy or your closest loved one!

The Cobra Man

The behavior of a cobra has a logic that makes it captive to its charmer; he easily holds it, to the gasps of the audience, without getting hurt, and the astonished viewer wonders: *Why doesn't the cobra change its routine behavior in order to escape its captivity and the abuses of its master?*

It appears mindless in front of its charmer as if spellbound or hypnotized. He toys with it, kisses it, and makes it dance as if a puppet on a stage; **it is captive not to a charmer who exploits it but rather to a logic that chains it, and it will never be free from the grasp of its charmer as long as it is not liberated from the captivity of the logic that controls its fate.** The charmer gained possession of the behavioral logic codes specific to that snake, rendering it in his hands a moving puppet!

The Cobra Man Draws Us

The scene of the cobra man is more complicated than it seems. We humans are also moving puppets, whether we're aware of it or not, and the cobra man earns money through drawing us in by our controlling strings to the seats of his stage and arena. The cobra man comes in many forms.

- **Commercial companies** attract consumers into buying a product they don't need or favoring an exorbitantly priced product over a cheaper and better product.

- **Politicians** attract people toward ideas that could be destructive or extremist.

- **Work managers** attract employees toward working for them for the cheapest and most austere prices.

Manufacturing Ciphers: The Skill of Giants

Giant companies and large international brands have the most control over human behavior, so what are the tactics of giants?

While small merchants have settled for taking advantage of the all-zeroes human cipher for the sake of reaping mutual interests and benefits through the buying and selling of products and services that consumers think they need, and within a framework of honest commercial competition in a free and balanced market in which risk and opportunity are commensurate…

Large corporations have gotten a craving for another devilish idea:

- **Why don't we manufacture a behavioral cipher** that can control consumers' behavior?

- **Why don't we market a "craze SIM"** which strikes people with mania?

- Rather than controlling a logic which we did not manufacture, and which is not completely loyal to us, **why don't we create a complexly encrypted attractive behavioral logic, loyal to our interests,** its secret codes in our hands, from which no maniac can escape?

The Human SIM

Giant companies are not satisfied by exploiting the breached ciphers of people to gain reasonable profits, but rather they take advantage of their vast resources to manufacture behavioral ciphers exclusive to them, more similar to a mobile phone's SIM card.

An Intercontinental Cipher

Giant companies spend billions on international marketing campaigns. An army of minds specialized in psychology, sociology, economics, politics, and programming communities. With their millions, they make international heroes and brilliant stars; they surround them with holy halos comparable to the holiness of a god in fans' psyches, and they use them in their plan to promote their holy ciphers through their concentrated advertisements and elaborate marketing campaigns, producing by these ciphers a human herd programmed for blind obedience.

The Herd Cipher

It creates a blind herd!

People leave high-quality and fairly priced products to madly converge on the brands of those shiny companies; they buy their products at many, many times the real price while proudly flaunting them.

They produce a herd eager for everything new, whose concern is the latest fad in the fashion world and the latest craze in the technology world.

They produce a herd whose family members all toil and work for the sake of catching up to the speedy fashion train; it spends all its money and reserves and borrows endless recurring loans for the sake of upgrading a car that's still new, exchanging a smartphone that's still shiny, or building a grand and towering house.

They produce a consumer herd that works ceaselessly and without rest, that eats not to live but lives to eat; they buy and consume just for the sake of buying and consuming.

The Cancer of Craziness

The crazes have spread even to the poorest and most remote areas of the world, where people live without shelter and suffer epidemics and famines. The epidemic of luxury and leisure and travel has spread like fire in the chaff of harvest, until the luxuries of luxuries have become life essentials, indispensable in the new logic of madness.

The "craze SIM" is a cancerous cipher manufactured by the giants' machine; it spreads the logic of madness and insanity amongst people.

These are scientific economic truths based on brand marketing foundations.

I am an economist, not a scriptwriter. This is not an imaginary film on conspiracies wrought against humanity; this is modern economics, which politicians and stars and athletes and economists and bank CEOs promote; all of them sing to the tune of opulence and splendor… puppets on a stage, all of them!

Think!

You hear of astronomical billions spent for the sake of controlling a growing company in the development stage.

What makes them spend all these billions in exchange for a losing company without profits?

Us simple folks count money in numbers, and they count in bank rolls and bundles and tons! **Where do they get all those tons?**

Don't worry, I promise you: I will not let you finish this book without a clear answer!

Tel Aviv-ian Bravery or Illogical Stupidity?

In 2000, I began work at the Tel Aviv branch of a CPA office. Like any other twenty-year-old, I was not sure if working in this office was what I was searching for and would fulfill my aspirations. I did not own a car, and direct transit from my town was unavailable, but I decided to try the job for a while. During that time, I shared a room with a friend of my brother's, in an apartment rented by four young men from the north part of the country who worked in the Central District. I practiced my forced settlement with them for a week, during which I slept on a floor mattress, feet bumping into me every morning, reminding me of my parasitism and making me feel embarrassed.

Driving a Car Without a Steering Wheel

I would come and go in a small broken-down car belonging to another friend of my brother's. Starting it up in the morning was a huge challenge. The degree of its swerve off the road was dangerous, and it required me to constantly keep the steering wheel in place with both my hands like someone riding a flighty horse. Driving it was complicated and avoiding crashing into another car was nigh impossible. Survival was purely accidental. I would feel its steering wheel coming out of its place as the car danced with me on the street.

The steering wheel was quick to separate, and I would force it in place the whole way. Each day I drove that car should have been the last adventure in my life, but despite this the fates willed otherwise. As I drove past an amusement park each day, I looked through the window in electrified terror toward the speedy death train within. What idiot would risk their life in such a careless manner?

A Youth Possessed

I returned to the apartment one day after surviving another car adventure, when I felt apprehension from one of the young men living with us. He was clutching the corner of the couch, his eyes transfixed in terror. It was as if he was in a staring contest with a terrifying monster. Wrapped in a blanket like a shield and clutching a cushion in his fist like a weapon, he shrank back nearly falling off the edge of the couch. My greeting was lost on him. Convinced the man was possessed, insane, or both, I looked toward my roommates for confirmation. None of them seemed to notice his affliction.

"What's wrong with him?" I asked.

My roommate answered without looking up from his work.

"He's just been watching a horror film, and he stays this way until the film ends. He's crazy!"

I turned around and saw that indeed the TV was on, albeit muted; he had not wanted to annoy the other residents of the apartment, and as soon as the film ended he pointed the remote to turn off the screen, and the "brave man" returned from the world of horror to this world, talking and joking and returning greetings as if his demon could be switched on and off with the remote.

Was he crazy or cowardly?

That young man taught me an extremely good lesson. He was truly brave. I would always avoid the roller coaster in the amusement park, and I never dared to ride it for fear of heights, and moreover for fear of people's laughing reactions; as for him, he had overcome two complexes in one scene.

Courage is not doing things you've gotten used to doing and which no longer scare you, even if that is fighting a lion!

I had risked driving a car no sane person would dare to drive, and that was not bravery on my part, nor did I feel like I was undertaking a dangerous, heroic act.

As for the young man, he had possessed enough internal courage to do something that shakes his limbs with fear, to the point that I thought for an instant he was insane, overcoming the fear of scary scenes and also liberating himself of the captivity of herd logic and the cowardice of fear of society's reactions. He had possessed the courage to watch the film to the end, and in front of the eyes of gloaters and ridiculers, without caring or being embarrassed or folding to the pressures, overcoming another complex.

This young man has leadership logic. Do you think that leaders are without feeling and take risks without fears clawing at them?

Fear is human nature; they just haven't allowed fear to take them captive.

When we look at ourselves and the people around us with an elastic, positive logic, we will discover that we have not noticed skills and valor that a rigid, negative logic had buried.

It Was I Who Was Crazy!

I had risked a whole week in taking a car in which the possibility of losing my life was the strongest hypothesis. Despite this, not even my eyelid fluttered, whereas merely the sight of the roller coaster from afar through the window of my crazy car struck me with an electric shivering, and without riding it. Even though if I had, it would have been safer than my uncontrollable car.

The wrong logic will lead you forcibly to an unreasonable path full of economic, societal, political, and domestic bumps which perhaps only a chance of fate will save you from!

So how do we escape from the captivity of our logic? And how do we understand others' logic?

You read and research and study for years in schools and colleges and universities in order to buy your freedom, and at the end of a long journey you discover that you've transformed from a simple slave to a cultured slave, and from a worker in a shirt into a worker in a necktie, and from a puppet on a stage to a puppet on a lectern or desk!

A Fantastic Reaction to the Events of a Film

We turn in an endless circular ring, going back to the beginning, in a life of gray landmarks, ruminating on the scenes of an old film, and the strange thing is we react to the events of the film as if we were living it for the first time. We treat it with the same behavior that caused us to perish the first time, and we practice the same failed reactions!

No one stops in the middle of the hall to leave or object or wonder, *Wait, what's happening here? We were in this scene before!*

True, some might wonder, but they quickly see the audience around them following the scene with the utmost attention, so they return to their seat again to watch the events of the repeated scene with yearning and eagerness!

A Military Example… A Genius Cipher

Military examples perhaps leave the clearest impression in human history because of their bloody consequences and regional impacts.

For example, Khalid ibn al-Walid[1] had such a genius as to let him never lose any of the battles he fought despite the small numbers with him, facing armies that outnumbered him an incomprehensible number of times, because, second to his deep and stubborn belief in his message, he possessed a complicated cipher to a crazy logic impossible for the enemy to decode or predict, and no common military convention followed his path.

He would take the enemy by surprise, inventing

---

1   An early Muslim commander who is considered in Islamic traditions to be one of the most accomplished generals. He is usually accredited for leadership and military tactics.

unprecedented military ways and that never occurred to the minds of the enemy generals; rather, they considered it insanity and an impossible adventure with uncalculated consequences.

On the other hand, he was a perceptive intelligence agent, easily uncovering the codes of the enemies' ciphers, so he would predict their movements and pauses as if they were pieces on a chess board, allowing him to easily and simply trap them in a variety of smart ambushes. He led them to where he wanted and fooled them whenever he wanted with whatever he wanted, so they approached their demise like puppets on a stage controlled by the strings of his genius.

When your logic is complexly encrypted and unexpected and your enemy's logic is uncovered to you, the war becomes one-sided, and victory is surely yours no matter how much stronger your enemy is!

It is a war of ciphers and minds, not only in military arenas but rather in all other life aspects without exception!

The Terrifying Incident of the Wasp's Nest

This incident nearly ended my life.

I was with my elder brother and my cousin, loitering in our neighbor's backyard. We often snuck out to swing in secret, amusing ourselves until our neighbors noticed. With a raised voice from our neighbor, we flew from the swing like acrobats.

Fleeing the Swings Became a Game of Risk

We were unable to resist the temptation, barely escaping each time. As soon as we heard the handle of the back door that looked out on the courtyard of the north field turn, we'd flee. Pushing each other onto a small path next to the house, we ran close to a wasp's nest. The path opened onto a southern concrete staircase which we leaped over or rolled until we came down to a front courtyard, running the length of it toward the external gate which looked onto the street. After we were at a safe distance, we celebrated. Our voices rose in screams and laughter.

Gargamel of the Smurfs

One time, our neighbor caught us awestruck, and I jumped off the swing at its zenith. I flew high in the air and was about to smack into a cement edge. My neighbor rushed to check on me as I twisted in pain. I discovered that day that our neighbor was not Gargamel of the Smurfs, and he did not have an evil cat in the house, just as our neighbor's wife was not a spellcasting witch.

Despite this, I continued to run with my peers, pushing and rolling in a dangerous fashion; and what could our neighbor do if he caught us? **The insanity of human logic starts from childhood!**

Cunning Discussions

And while we were loitering in the narrow west path, the wasps flying around a hole in the corner of a wall of old stones arrested us; my older brother and cousin discussed around throwing a stone to the hole and running toward the exit stairs, but they quickly changed their minds for fear of the wasps' terrifying chase!

A Sudden Attack

While I was close to the nest, my cousin threw the stone from a distance without prior warning and fled with my brother following him, and the wasp colony's rage was roused…

In a moment, I thought that my following them to the outside would expose me to certain danger because I was the last, and the raging wasps would fill me with stings instead of them, because they would think that I was the evildoer, so I cunningly planned to escape to the rear courtyard so that the wasps could chase the perpetrators as they pleased; those two were fast and would surely survive.

My childish reading of the wasps' logic was naive and stupid, because the wasps left them to escape and chased the nearest target. They did not care who had thrown the stone; their instinctive raging logic made them tear me apart with stings as I twisted in the dirt from the pain of the swellings until my body was numbed and I no longer felt the pricks!

Oblivious in a Place of Riot

I was as a poor oblivious innocent who had happened to pass by a place of riot, so the soldiers turned on him with their batons from all sides, and he cried pleading for mercy with no one answering. Their stings nearly killed me; then I felt someone's hand supporting me and his other small hand vigorously hitting me, driving away and killing the wasps that were sticking to my body and neck and head and repeating their stings with the insistence of vengeance and without mercy or pity. I had no more power to resist, my face swelled, and my jugulars pulsed with poisons!

But it was my brother who had returned by the kind and courageous logic of brotherhood to save his younger brother, exposing himself to the wasps' stings, and he supported me until we reached home.

The Bicycle Split

Since we did not have a car at home, my mother instructed my brother to hastily take me on the back of his bicycle to the town's clinic, saying she would follow us on her feet, and there they swiftly received me and my brother with quick treatments and antivenom shots. Then we returned home exhausted with pricks and shots.

And on our way home, the bicycle broke into two halves in the middle, as if that was all that was needed. So, we each picked up a half and stumbled along, I supported my brother and he supported me; we carried it instead of it carrying us!

The Ciphers of the Wasps and My Cousin

The wasps' behavior had a logic I failed to uncover, which made me an easy prey, and this was a practical, applicable lesson which revealed to me the world of behavioral ciphers at a very early age, and in a way that was nearly fatal. Solving the logical equation would have allowed me to escape and control events, but I failed to uncover the cipher of my cousin's behavior first, and the wasps' behavior second!

Your Compounded Duty

The danger of my failure was not limited to myself, but extended to my brother as well, who rushed to help me by the logic of kindness and bravery which led him to save me.

Our successes and failures often reach those around us and affect our families, and this is what compounds our duty and drives us to understand logic and uncover its secrets, attracting prosperity and benefits and shielding from evils and abuses, for our sakes and for the sakes of those in our orbits.

I Don't Sell You Nonsense

But, so we can be realistic, it's true that uncovering the secrets and codes gives you the tool that allows you to take control of the reins of your life, and even to control the reins of others and of the world, **but that will never happen as long as you don't have the desire and the courage to do that.**

Personally, I was more afraid of the roller coaster ride than I was fearful of risky ventures. My absolute certainty that riding the roller coaster in the amusement park would not bring me any harm did not help me; I preferred a trade deal with a certain loss over undertaking an acrobatic experience with certain survival-- rather I even drove a car that only a strange fate saved me from by a weird chance.

People are all like this; they hide in themselves in fear of some particular thing which prevents them from moving toward a logical behavior that might be their only lifesaver.

Being intelligent does not make you a successful leader.

It's not enough for us to be convinced nor for us to understand the truth and know the way, or to uncover the encrypted codes, since how would someone who doesn't have the courage and the desire to touch a dead or drugged cobra be able to kiss it while it's alive and moving? Because even if he had the secrets of snake charming and learned them, he will never use them, and they will not benefit him!

Because of this you could find him:

- **One of the biggest economics consultants**

- **One of the biggest psychiatric consultants**

- **One of the biggest educational consultants**

And the greatest successful people and giants of the market eagerly and fervently snatch up his consultative

services, but he does not apply them to his reality and does not take advantage of them to his benefit. He remains merely a shadow or unknown soldier, not because he is ignorant and does not know, but because he is captive to a logic that he knows is incorrect; however, he does not have the daring and desire.

An Example Recorded by the Holy Books

The historical story of the Israelites with Moses peace be upon him serves as an ideal example of a people whose Lord had promised them an assured victory by simply entering the holy land, but they were too cowardly to even attempt it; they suggested to their prophet that he go with his Lord to fight alone, even though they had just tried at his hands miracles that drowned Pharaoh, the alleged god of Egypt, and delivered them from his tyranny in a fashion that broke the scientific laws of the universe. Thus followed the Exodus - **40 years wandering the Earth!**

The Secret of 40

What's striking and scary in the story of the Exodus is the number 40; the wrong logic cost the Israelites 40 valuable years wandering in the desert. **They move without pause; they don't settle in one place or state and their mind cannot rest. They drink and eat and sleep and die, their night is as their day and their today identical to their yesterday, lost in a vicious cycle and swimming in an orbit.**

Doesn't that scene seem familiar?

Doesn't that scene seem familiar in your life or in the life of most people? Repeat after me and activate your imagination: *They revolve without pause; they don't settle in one place and don't remain in one state and their mind cannot rest. They drink and eat and sleep and die, their night is as their day and their today identical to their yesterday, lost in a vicious cycle and swimming in an orbit!*

This is the grave secret!

The wrong logic could lead you into a long exodus in your life that could last 40 springs of your lifetime. You turn and turn and turn around the mill of failure or routine to reach the autumn of age worn out by failed experiences and misguided attempts without applying the lessons and absorbing the morals from the simplest situations of your life. You have continued to chase after a distant mirage, leaving behind the low-hanging fruit.

Save 40 Years

This is what I am trying to make clear for you through my book, in order to save for you 40 valuable years of your limited life.

Life is simple and beautiful.

But the wrong human logic practices intimidation and scare tactics on us, making our life seem harsh and complicated; our weak point is the fear of the unknown, and our incorrect logic exploits the fear complex in us in order to safeguard its position and keep us captive until we die!

He that Lives with Cripples Learns to Limp

And when 40 years have passed over a man captive in a cell with mice, he becomes a mouse in the clothes of a man, unless he has a tough pioneering leadership logic made of reinforced steel; and as they say, he who keeps company with the wolves will learn to howl.

Grants and Gifts Along the Way

During our lifetimes, we go through life experiences that could be extreme at times, whether in pain or delight. These are grants and gifts driven to us, or we to them, so that we can correct a flawed logic or gain a new one upon which we plan our next destination, toward a summit that awaits us.

The Israelites' Logic

The abundance of miracles that the Israelites witnessed and their passage through the depths of the sea parted by Moses' extraordinary staff gained them an incorrect logic by which their lives strayed; for 40 years they were lost!

Those miracles were driven to them to let them gain a precious behavioral logic which Moses called them to; he wanted them to have confidence in his Lord when they had beheld His care and gentleness toward them and witnessed His power and might over their enemy.

It was reasonable that those sights would have gained them a deep belief, blind obedience, and confidence in the Lord's commands and interdictions!

But they contrived a logic contrary to the one that was willed for them:

They depended without trying instead of relying on God while doing what was asked of them, and followed the path of cowardly logic, to which they became habituated for many long years in the humiliation of captivity.

The logic of cowardice crippled them and embellished for them the idea that the Lord is omnipotent, as they had just seen miracles and marvels, of which their eyes and their hands and their feet could bear witness; rather, even their clothes which they crossed the sea in without getting wet can bear witness, but their logic told them: Stay still here!

The logic of cowardice, or more specifically the logic of miracles, which the Israelites adopted was unrealistic and unreasonable.

Divine Interventions

Medical miracles or extraordinary wonders could be driven to you, saving you from a deeply dark ending or a fate of certain demise. Divine providence always grants you a second and third and fourth "chance" so that every time you get mired in a life predicament which no logical trick can help with, how quickly an amazing divine grant snatches you from its quagmire, coming to you as if by chance!

This is what the Israelites sorely needed when they reached the rock bottom of weakness and the base of humiliation and complete loss of confidence… their critical condition required extraordinary resuscitative miracles!

Some might consider these grants to be miracles wrought by nature or chances driven by good luck; as for the Israelites who had become used to humiliation, they explained these marvels with the logic of cowardice which they had become habituated to over the years that they had spent in the captivity of torture and slavery.

The Calf of Extraordinary Logic

Logical human experiences could not have saved and liberated them from that intractable complex, so God sent them extraordinary experiences and astonishing miracles, and even then they did not leave the bondage of the god of cowardly logic that had enslaved them!

And the logic of cowardice that they idolized deceived them, and it extracted for them from the summation of those miracles the statue of a calf that had a lowing sound, "the calf of extraordinary logic", and they said, 'this is your god, and the god of Moses".

Even miracles might not convince a "slave" to the wrong logic!

Even miracles did not make them realize that the fault was in the logic they had let direct their life. They had seen the magic staff do everything and did not see Moses' hand which moved the staff by the Lord's command.

Instead of gaining the logic of courage, which would cast into them the confidence that with them is a power that will never let them down, and the certainty that Pharaoh despite his deification was only a human, and the conviction that they are now free people with dignity, they surrendered to the ramming horns of the rampant logic, and all those lessons and marvels were not successful in giving life to a dormant body and a spent confidence!

And they insisted on worshipping a calf that gave neither harm nor benefit.

Rather, on the contrary, they worshipped the calf of extraordinary logic, bowing their heads saying:

Here, the marvels and miracles are no longer impossible, so why should we tire and toil and battle when we have an extraordinary god who says to something be and it is, and between our hands is the staff of marvels that splits the sea and cuts rivers and devours what they falsify[2]?

---

2   Quran 7:117 "And We inspired to Moses, 'Throw your staff,' and at once it devoured what they were falsifying."

It is the logic that idolizes marvels and counts on luck and miracles; it discouraged them, and they said to their prophet, **"Go, you and your Lord, and fight. Indeed, we are remaining right here!"[3]**

The Logic of Marvels and the Complex of The Guided One[4]

Many people sit and wait for a divine miracle to accomplish difficult missions for them. The doctrine or complex of the awaited Guided One has enticed them; they walk the same path and take the same lanes and ride the same trains then hope to open their eyes onto a brighter morning and happier news and a better life and a more beautiful reality.

It reminds me of the mouse,

Yes, the mouse in Spencer Johnson's *Who Moved my Cheese?* They remind me of that mouse.

I will summarize the story of that mouse in my own way; in reality it is the story of the little person and not the mouse, but allow me to switch the roles to make the idea apparent:

The giant piece of cheese disappeared; the mouse had gotten used to finding it every day in its place in the cheese cellar. He

---

3   Quran 5:24

4   The Guided One, or Mahdi, is an Islamic figure widely believed to be a future redeemer who will fight against the Antichrist and rid the world of evil.

and his friend would eat from it to excess and came to depend on it. And one day, they did not find it; their hearts jumped out from terror. They returned the next day and the mouse opened his eyes, and his heart broke anew when he did not find the piece of cheese. On the third day, he flew again to the storeroom hoping to find it, and was surprised again, and he lived captive between the walls of conceit turning in a vicious cycle, opening his eyes and closing them, sleeping and waking up, asking, "Who moved my cheese?" He had practiced the highest degrees of optimism to the point that he could nearly touch the cheese mirage in his daydreams. As for his friend, he had decided at last to search for the cheese in another place and a new cellar, and he succeeded!

Before the White Strand of Hair Appears

When we analyze our behaviors, we find that many people have the same unrealistic behavior as that mouse. He did not move or change ways. He had practiced optimism in the wrong fashion; closing your eyes with great optimism then opening them will not change anything in your reality.

When you're not ready to renounce your logical god, then you will never dare to fundamentally change, and you will continue to hover and hover around your flawed holy complex.

Some have dressed their flawed logic in a new divine dress, thinking that the fault was decorative, and that an incorrect belief could be renovated and corrected with some scents and paints; **they said: No doubt the secret lies in how strongly I shut my eyes!**

Therefore, you see them shut their eyes again for a longer time and with greater pressure, then open their eyes and are surprised that the dream did not come true. They close their eyes again and squeeze with great optimism and the result is the same without change; they close and open their eyes, open and close, wake and sleep, sleep and wake… and are surprised and disappointed each time!

And one time they come eagerly with another decorative dress, after 40 years of failed experiences: **Perhaps the secret is in how fast I shut my eyes?**

Don't be hasty; that wasn't a totally naive idea. And indeed, they stand in front of the mirror and shut their eyes and open them quickly. They stare into the mirror and oh, to their great astonishment and the terror of surprise, this time something new has appeared after long waiting:

No, the awaited Guided One has not appeared, but… a white strand of hair has!

If you want to accompany me to the end:

Renounce the divinity of logic, and come with me step by step, before the white strand of hair appears.

A Young Teenage Logic

Sometimes even miracles are not helpful in solving a complexity whose foundation is a habitual incorrect logic, and this is what gives a plausible explanation for a crazy behavioral logic, such as idolatry, which was and still is widespread in some form or another.

And are idolaters the only example of disbelievers?

Before I opened my own office, I used to leave for my accounting job in Tel Aviv after dawn prayer directly or a little before. I had reached a position that let me freely choose my hours and workdays, going early and returning early, avoiding the choking traffic jams; because instead of reaching within less than forty-five minutes, the road would have cost me at times three hours if I were to be late in leaving or returning.

Harassments in the Street

But sleeping late and waking early nearly killed me more than once. My driving logic was insanely adolescent. Several times I fell asleep at the wheel of my red sports car, with its glass convertible roof and magnesium rims; I would be startled awake by angry warning horns or the rumbling of the alert strips as my car swerved and almost crushingly hugged an approaching trailer truck, or gotten too close to an adjacent car, or accidentally harassed the car in front, or perhaps skidded down a cliff without a protective rail!

The drowsiness would fly off me at the force of the terror that would strike me; the adrenaline shock of fear would supply me with a few minutes of caution and alertness, but how soon it would quickly fade away, and my eyes would begin to droop again.

A Kissing Distance

One time, as I was returning home from work in the afternoon, I was tearing along in my red car like a drunkard, approaching a line of cars in a traffic jam at the entrance of the Israeli town of Bat-Hefer, shortly before the Arab village of Zemer, and near my city West Baqa.

You could see me speeding toward the line at full speed like a blind man; I was awake but absentminded, and in a sudden heavenly moment I noticed the disaster. I slammed on my brakes frantically trying to avoid the cars, the sharp, high screeching of the brakes sounding like the whinny of a horse on a battlefield. I saw the eyes of the driver in front of me staring into his mirror with a panicked gaze, speechless from the severity of the screech and the strength of my car's push toward his vehicle carrying him and his family. By a miracle, the car stopped at kissing distance from sure collision. The blood pounded in my veins and my face reddened, and the looks watching me could not believe that my car had stopped. I stole a glance toward the man's vehicle to see him and his family breathing heavily, and the smell of rubber pervaded the scene.

The Paralytic Logic of Miracles

We may blame the Israelites and not blame ourselves for miracles or wonders that block our path and whip us so that we can change our behavior. They are free lessons that God drives to us through chance!

I nearly died several times without changing my behavior. A backwards logic was leading me; all I cared about was that I did not wait in traffic, without noticing the dangers or the repeated miracles that saved my life. I had become used to these miracles, so I no longer cared for the dangers, and continued to take – or rather, that same logic continued to take me and drive me and lead me and enslave me, and I waited for the next miracle to save me for sure.

The Logic of Road Accidents

One of my adolescent peers was killed in a terrifying traffic accident at the beginning of his life on his way to work, and even that was ineffective in changing my behavior. Traffic accidents continue to harvest human lives, without stopping and without a reasonable logic, all this despite awareness workshops and traffic safety education campaigns.

This is an example of the power of incorrect logic which no advice, stinging ear-twist, deadly life experience, or extraordinary miracle may be effective against.

Are We Predestined?

Some paralyzed wisecrack of those who follow the dependency logic will jump up to prove on these traces that we are predestined, and that we have no choice in controlling our miserable, poor reality and suicidal, dangerous behavior, and that we must wait for a miracle or wonder.

No, that is not the reasonable objective, just as it was not Moses' (peace be upon him) objective that the Israelites should lean on the major miracles that they witnessed become reality with a frequency that has never been repeated in human history as it was repeated in front of a viewer or listener amongst them. **So, they took to sleep and resignation; rather, their rudeness reached the point of asking their prophet that he take the hand of his Lord and go with him to the battlefront.**

No, we are not forced.

Rather, go back to the details of your life. You will find that they were practical lessons and behavioral morals freely driven to you as they were driven to me, but you chose, as I chose, to ignore them and interpret them according to a sleeper mindset. And we let that incorrect logic control our ways and paths, grazing in the valley of the slackers, turning in the orbit of danger, and licking the wounds of poverty and need and failure.

Luck is a Curse on the One Who Encounters It

Does luck accompany the successful? Or do successful people accompany luck? Who searches for the other?

This is like the question of the chicken and the egg: which came first?

And it is neither a scientific nor a logical question, because the existence of the chicken or the existence of the egg are extraordinary miracles, in contradiction to the foundations of science and beyond the limits of the mind, so going into it is a waste of time and effort.

We ought to always search for practical solutions, instead of inventing excuses for our misery; you will never find a successful person attributing their success to a stroke of luck, but you will find unsuccessful people justifying their failure by saying that luck avoids them and attributing the success of others to luck being on their side.

What is the secret of luck's alliance with the rich and successful?

The leadership explanation leads us to a nice, beneficial, and encouraging explanation by which we can understand the ways of luck and its policies:

In truth, luck does not follow anyone; it only walks the trails of leadership, loiters in the gardens of optimism, and inhabits the places of courage that leaders frequently patronize.

The Sting of Death

Therefore, leaders are susceptible to luck smiling and bestowing itself upon them, more than those pessimists and laggards, whom a strange chance might lead to randomly collide with luck's parade at the intersection of the road of misery they're on day and night, so its meeting with them is for the most part a disastrous collision accident. Fortune may smile upon them as is its habit but by way of courtesy or cunning; it gifts them the sting of death dressed as a kiss which they think is the chance of a lifetime.

When luck smiles upon leaders, they gain increased success and happiness and wealth, and they may reencounter luck in the places they are in; it welcomes them with elation and glee, adding to their spoils and successes.

On the other hand, statistics prove that those who are lucky by way of arbitrary encounters are not of those who have a courageous leadership logic, such as athletic stars who reap enormous fortunes in the millions, or the impoverished who win the lottery, or thieves who rob a bank, or traitors who embezzle an organization, or scoundrels who have become skilled in crime; they quickly go bankrupt and descend into hardship and poverty and debt and addiction, and they may reach the rock bottom of suicide because of the poisoned kiss of luck.

Why do we know but not attain?

Intelligence is not sufficient to gain you a leadership logic, nor is knowing and learning and studying books, nor is joining workshops and seminars,

You might gain a scientific fortune for the sake of general knowledge or earning a livelihood or social prestige, but there is a vast difference between the logic of knowledge and behavioral logic. You could grab knowledge by its lapels, but it will not give you anything of the world of leadership, because you did not crystallize a new logic for you based on your stores of knowledge.

You need of a correct behavioral doctrine so that you can learn, not play around!

Someone might peruse the world of theology or study the science of comparative religion, not to reach a truth or sound doctrine, but for scientific extravagance, or cultural clashes, or revengeful logic, or a fanatical bias.

Training or Tickles?

When we give our behavioral logic dogmatic holiness, the sciences and training seminars become merely emotional tickles and momentary psychological revolutions which quickly die down and render you an obedient slave to that corrupt behavioral doctrine which we have let impose its authority with all clout and arrogance.

- **How else do you explain the logic of a nutritionist who advises you with a dietary regimen**, when she herself needs three emergency programs to save her from obesity?

- **Or how do you explain the logic of a cardiologist who admonishes you to quit smoking**, while he imbibes a cigarette, blowing its poisons in your face?

- **Or how do you explain the logic of a father who admonishes his son to avoid lying**, then tells him to tell the caller: My father is not home?

A Rare Answer from the Man of Rarities

As for my uncle, he had a personal logic on the topic of smoking; when an adviser admonished him to quit because it harms health and wastes money, my uncle answered him:

"I know better about my health and my money. **As for health:** my age has exceeded eighty-six; no doctor has examined me, I've never been to a hospital, and I climb trees to harvest olives. **And as for money:** I plant Arabic tobacco in my field, taking from the yield what I need and selling the excess for my livelihood."

The adviser did not expect this rare answer from the man of rarities, so he left him and went on his way!

An Incorrect Logic of a 90-year-old

This uncle of mine has reached 90 years old today, and has formed his personal logic which he has contrived from his exceptional circumstances and rare condition. His long life is rare even amongst his brothers and sisters; most of them have passed despite their young age. His oldest son also recently died, and even so, it is difficult or nearly impossible to argue with him or convince him to change a logic which, for ninety years, has not let him down!

Logic: Something has proved itself, so why change it?

When we survive time after time, even if by luck or chance or miracle, we feel secure in the logic or strategy we followed, which is what might make some consider their logic a constant scientific truth or an indisputable or uncriticizable law; something has proved itself, so why should we change it?

The Demon of "You Can Tempt Providence and always Win"

This does not differ from the behavior of teenagers, or my behavior when I was driving a car whose steering wheel was almost coming loose or driving my car drowsy and miracles recurring for me, when I would be startled awake before my death by a breath every time.

I did not change my crazy behavior, even though my survival was fraught with hidden wonders, and even though the blows were buffeting me and shaking me so I could wake up and change in order to survive before it was too late!

Because I had gotten used to and coexisted with the reality of "you can tempt fate and triumph" coming true and repeating, and I would return home safe again, until I surrendered to this corrupt doctrine, **and the logic of "you can tempt fate and triumph" became a demon dominating me and a holy verse driving me!**

A Struggle Between the Scientific Mind and Tried Reality

When the reasonable scientific mind collides with an observable self-logic, for the most part and unconsciously, we let the perceptible logic lead our steps, even if it were an incorrect logic contradictory to science and the reasonable.

That's because humans by nature lean toward the familiar, even if it's a logic surrounded by dangers or a cause of their hardships and miseries; and they fear the unknown which they are unfamiliar with, even if it's proven science and validated scientific reality.

Smart of Mind, Stupid of Logic

Being successful, rich, or happy does not mean you are smart. We hear sayings such as **"God gives meat to one without teeth"** or **"He gives an earring to one without ears"**; this is a wrong conclusion springing from the crooked logic that controls the behavior of the speaker.

Someone could be stupid or ignorant in your view but could have a leadership logic that submits to their command.

They control their logic without letting it overtake them.

Because they continuously correct their logic, submitting it to criticism and polishing it with a meager quantity of the knowledge and experiences that they gain, taking advantage of every fact however simple and every experience however fleeting and every saving wonder.

They don't give their behavioral logic a chance to become deified or to grow its horns, and they don't let it take a halo that matches belief and exceeds the holiness of the Lord, as with Moses' lost companions.

Science in the Service of a False God

This is the difference between a leader who controls the lapels of his logic and does not consecrate it and between a scientist or smart person whose behavioral logic controls him as a god who cannot be disobeyed or opposed.

The smart person and the scientist face life experiences and facts by the tons, which they offer as sacrifices on the altar of worshipped behavioral logic; then all these facts kneel prostrating in service to that despotic logic and nourish its ramming horns.

The Fission Equation

The pollination of science with leadership logic gives birth to a universal fission equation, the extent of whose effects on your life and society and the whole world are unpredictable.

In general, leaders are not the smartest people; they realize this well, which is what makes them always search for the services of the strongest minds, and they spend money to attract smart brains to their sides with the goal of constructing the monoliths of their empires.

Hold it by its horns!

Renounce the divinity of the behavioral logic that governs you. Pull it down by force from your throne and place it on the dissection table; break its horns, set its limits, and define its role for it, and keep your eyes on its horns so they don't grow again.

Only then will you taste the flavor of freedom, and life will smile on you. You will take command of the channels of your present and future in order to control your domestic, daily, and social life as if you had been reborn.

Taste freedom so you can get to where you want, not where it wants!

When you are freed, all your simple life experiences become the most beautiful tale, the most amazing tune, and the best moral and most eloquent lesson. You will dominate it, not it you, so you can get to where you want to get, not where it wants to get you to.

The Magical Dieting Recipe

Slenderness is perhaps one of the topics that worries young girls especially, and fatness and obesity remain a global pandemic threatening the health of young and old. I have had a successful personal experience that allowed me to reduce my weight by about 20 kilograms, or 44 lbs. during a period of only three months, keeping up my achievement for years without resorting to advertised programs.

I did it quickly, which caught the attention of many of those around me. The looks would prey on me wherever I went; I would notice the looks of amazement and astonishment in their eyes.

One of the acquaintances, who was my father's age, stopped me in the mosque after a year and asked me: My son, I've been wanting to ask you since some time ago, but by God I did not want to be nosy. You're like my son as you know, and I only want to be reassured about you; are you suffering from a disease that made you get this lean?

I smiled and reassured him that I had only been self-dieting; he reluctantly believed me and went on his way.

Two Difficult Years!

I spent two difficult years, looks of suspicion and pity following me wherever I came and went, and to this day whoever meets me asks me: Are you suffering from anything? Have you undergone a gastric bypass or gastric band surgery?

I tell them that I had only practiced a self-diet, but everyone could hardly believe me. Every time summer arrived, and I wore tight clothes, they asked me the same questions again; their imaginations still held the image of me when I was fat.

My Personal Program

My program was simple and logical; I reduced the amount of food I was eating for about two months, and after my weight stopped decreasing, I began to exercise daily for a whole month; the matter doesn't need magical programs.

Far away from modern nutrition terminology, the simple logic is clear: If you put in your mouth less than usual your weight drops, and if you exercise, you burn the extra food that entered, period!

Despite this, people's logic has deviated; they chase after programs and recipes in all areas of the world, and they hardly believe that someone could lower their weight like this without an incurable illness or a surgical operation or secret program or magical substance. Even those who undergo a surgical operation quickly gain weight again; one of my friends repeated the operation again!

The 30/30 Program: Lose 30 Kilograms in One Month

You see them chasing after the mirage of ridiculous advertisements: **"Lose 30 kilogram in 30 days, while eating what you want, and even without exercising"**; what is this nonsense they're selling? What disbelieving logic is this that calls you to deny science and believe in fraud and run after the mirage of deceit in this obvious manner!

When the wrong logic leads us, we fail to see validated truths and available chances and profitable deals and keep running after a mirage!

Let me repeat an earlier point: Life is much simpler than we imagine, and the realization of success is much easier than we picture; there is no need for wonders and over-philosophizing and oversaturated programs.

The Mind or Logic: What Moves Us?

We don't move on our own. Logic is what moves everyone, and here is where the danger lies in if the codes of your personal logical cipher fall into hands which could lure you toward a terrific exploitation or take you to an arena which could be where you meet your end; how dangerous it is for your logic to be wrong, or your cipher breached!

Rather, what's more dangerous is that your cipher be manufactured by an opponent or a giant of the market.

A Different Logic = A Different Way = A Different Result

There is a logic that moves the rich and a logic that moves the poor, a logic that moves the successful and a logic that moves the failing, a logic that moves the masters and a logic that moves the slaves, and a logic that moves the courageous and a logic that moves the cowards!

There is no one logic in the universe, or else everyone would be following the same pattern, rich or poor and successful or failing and masters or followers; but for each one there is a logic that leads their steps to a destiny.

Doesn't that seem naive?

Okay, I am not that naive; it's impossible for everybody to be masters because there are no masters without slaves, and God has favored some people above others so that life can be straight and roles complementary. There are boss and bossed, manager and employee, scientist and merchant, and farmer and craftsman.

But that doesn't lessen the importance and power of secrets and codes, and it does not cancel their ability to turn your life and future head over heels.

Realizing the secret and solving the codes grant you magical tools and an extraordinary weapon, but these tools will never benefit you so long as you don't possess the desire to use a unique destructive weapon and the courage to ride the express train from your familiar world to a strange world.

You need a sound behavioral doctrine to breach the impossible!

The Clash of the Poles of Logic

The poor consider the logic of the rich a crazy adventure, while the rich consider the logic of the poor a crazy suicide.

In every world of our economic, social, and political worlds, there are poles that see the other pole as crazy, so which of them is crazy? Which of them is the dominator and which of them is the dominated?

A Puppet in the Hand of a Scoundrel Who Moves You Towards a Plastic Carrot

We can discover the deepest and most complicated secrets that hold dominion over our lives; these secrets are scattered in our daily realities and activities, past and present. By deciphering their codes, we can liberate ourselves from their ever-present and insidious control. When we do so, we will lead ourselves instead of being led by others.

You will be astonished when you realize that all this time you have only been a puppet in the hand of a scoundrel who moves you toward a plastic carrot.

"Scoundrel" is not a rude description... remember what economists say:

They don't say it explicitly, but what they really say is: we humans are scoundrels in our nature, and this is neither an insult nor a compliment. Rather, it is the reality of humans. They are a cluster of opportunistic benefits that does not move except toward a benefit and only walks on the tracks of the logic of insanity. We search for a paradise or flee from a hellfire, and we search for a hope or flee from pain, and we search for profit or flee from loss, and search for approval or flee from displeasure, and search for survival or flee from demise!

However perceptible or imperceptible the goal is, and material or abstract, and religious or conscientious, then it is a pure self-benefit; if not for benefit you would not have moved from your place. That very same benefit that moved you some people's logic might consider valuable, and others' logic will consider it worthless.

Certainly, you don't get up early in the morning to go to your factory because you think of the benefit of the people working for you, and the worker does not get up early in the morning because he is thinking of the benefit of your factory, even if the automatic outcome is the running of the factory and its success.

For each one of you is a graph describing your benefits; economists try hard to find a mathematical expression for this complicated drawing that is governed by material and immaterial and apparent and hidden and logical and illogical. Your benefits - yours and your worker's - have met at an intersection point which is the factory that you own.

You will be shocked when I tell you that you don't donate to someone except for your personal benefit; no doubt that you ask for an unseen paradise or divine pleasure or heart's bliss or social recognition.

Perhaps the scene of that poor person upset your feelings or pricked your conscience, so you moved to rest your conscience, and this too is a benefit for you, as you have pushed away from yourself the harm of the pricks and brought to yourself a psychological cheer… whatever the benefit, it comes back to you!

The Mouse Man

Something fantastical that nearly gave me an epileptic fit – I swear to you thrice I'm not kidding or lying; it was not magic. I saw a hulk forcing himself into a mouse hole whose size did not exceed 10 centimeters in length, width and height!

I don't know why or how, and don't ask me to cover myself well before sleeping, nor for someone to pinch me; it was real. I have clips documenting the event and proving the case.

I tracked down the man. He had lived a miserable life in captivity between four walls among the mice of the cell. His whole life he watched the rats until he mastered that strange art.

- He is a **genius** who possesses a mind that qualifies him to lead the world, but he's chained in a job that doesn't make ends meet.

- He is a talented **athlete** in an obsolete team but switching to a well-known team doesn't occur to him.

- He is an **innovator** who abandons his innovations and spends his time working on the bus.

- He is a brilliant **merchant**, but he spends his life selling at traffic lights.

- He is a **worker** with rare skills, and he doesn't think of a project or job that suits him.

He is that same mouse man who got used to the logic of mice, so it led him voluntarily to the hole of poverty and need.

It is you and me when we possess skills and abilities but accept the logic of lowliness.

The Logic of Destructions: Examples That Destroy Nations and Kill Motivations

The danger is compounded because most people have a breached hereditary logic, or one that is unencrypted to begin with, open to experienced and inexperienced merchants and to the proprietors of interests and the owners of economies. They are aware of your movements and predict them exactly, which makes you susceptible to extortion and undervaluation, because they know that your cipher is of poverty and cowardice and need, and that your logic is: *Cutting off necks rather than cutting off livelihoods, Give me wool today and take a sheep tomorrow, If there was any good in it, the bird wouldn't have dropped it, Tire your body and don't tire your heart...*

These are proverbs that reinforce the logic of imitation and subordination and legislate the logic of the herd.

Don't Deprive the World

- On the basis of these inherited axioms, you might not dare to change your profession or place of work, for fear of losing your livelihood, as if it were the life-giving oxygen tube, and in preference for the crumbs in your hand.

- And on the same basis, you might not choose a university major that you will excel in or a technical craft that you'll be brilliant in because you were afraid of the job market that everyone warned you about and how few people are in the field, so you deprive yourself and your society and perhaps the whole world of a golden chance to benefit from your genius.

- And in the same manner, you might kill the giant innovator living in the depths of your little son and daughter, and you demotivate them and paralyze their dream; so you only see us give birth to clones of ourselves who orbit around the epicenter of our cowardly logic.

And in this way, you deprive yourself and your family and your society and the world from your reserved pearls.

Let's not rush to conclusions before their time.

Together, we have plunged into a gain that has fried your brain, scrambled your insides, and made your thinking go haywire. Pressing on a pain increases the pain, but it's necessary for a sure diagnosis, so that we can choose the effective treatment.

We have really begun to solve the codes and loosen the roots of the rigid logic.

And now the time has come…

To reveal the mask of spells and clearly decipher the codes and regain control again, to set forth from this moment to wherever we want…

Come with me to find that which has been missing all your lifetime, and here you are waiting on tenterhooks for it so that the solution of the mystery of your life can be complete!

ACT

DECIPHERING THE CODES

Diagnosis and Identifying the Pain Point

You have just been shown the obscure world of ciphers. Together, we can solve the complex that you used to run into all your life, which caused you to fall flat in defeat.

Choose: The Cobra Man or the Mouse Man?

And we just saw as well how the cobra man took control of the logical codes of the deadly cobra and as such captured it, and led the audience to his stage, while the mouse man was captured by mouse logic which led him to his small hole.

Who would you prefer to be… the cobra man or the mouse man?

The majority dream of being the cobra man, yet they practice the logic of the mouse man, satisfied by life in the holes.

You Attack Enthusiastically Like a Stormy Wave Then Break

How many times have you launched attacks and fierce motivational campaigns that you would plunge into after reading a provocative book or watching an encouraging clip or listening to an inspirational story, and each time you break and your fervor dies down? **When you try and vow to…**

- **change your reality, life, and behavior.**

- **be nicer to your wife and kids.**

- **be more enthusiastic and meticulous in your work.**

- **improve your interest or trade.**

- **start executing your project and idea.**

- **gain a professional, artistic, or life skill.**

- **exercise or become physically fit.**

- **adhere to a nutritional plan and healthy diet.**

You try and vow and get enthusiastic, and actually begin preparing, and you might announce a sweeping attack, but then you break, and the flame of your enthusiasm dies down; you regress, dragging the tails of disappointment and defeat behind you.

Surrendering despite possessing the tools, experiences, and skills

How plentiful are failed campaigns, announced and engaged in by many; then the strikes of cowardice and failure don't take long to cripple them time after time.

Until a person is struck with despair and stops trying and surrenders, despite his possession of all the tools, experiences, and skills that qualify him for victory and triumph.

Let's decipher the symbols of that insanity together!

We began the process of loosening the roots of incorrect logic, and now we will pull those roots out from their base and decipher all the codes.

Logic is a Human Invention

Logic is a human invention; it is a tyrannical overlord and a devastating captor, like a vortex that drags in the drowning or a magical staff for sleepers or a spell that chains idiots. It is not a universal law that cannot be trespassed on or argued with, but we fear its power and dread questioning it, and we avoid trespassing on it or challenging it.

And when we come face-to-face with an event that breaches logic or collide with truths that challenge the delusion of that deluded logic and reveal its flaws to the eyes, we say that this is an illogical event and a fact that opposes logic… **the insanity of humans is unbelievable!**

There is nothing in the world that is illogical; there is an incorrect and crooked logic.

And there is no logical or illogical law; it's either a law or a logic!

Because logic is outside the bounds of established laws, because it's a hypothesis yet to be proven, and it could be absurd or random. When logic becomes proven, it is no longer a logic and has become a scientific fact or universal law.

Until you absolutely prove the validity of a logic, it remains a hypothesis to be researched and discussed; we should not blindly submit to it without thinking. As long as a logic is not absolutely proven and does not have definitive evidence, it will never be a law except only in your imaginative delusions.

And was there a logic that made the rational, adult man that we met in the Second Act live in a mouse hole?

"The Adventures of Auster, King of the Ostriches"

"Auster" of the ostriches tells you of a stranger logic than that; he sticks his head into a grand palace, waving his wings in the air while his legs dance rapturously in the open.

"Auster" is not an ordinary ostrich; he is the founding king and the greatest of the kingdom of ostriches. He had just returned from an official visit to the kingdom of mice, famous for its palaces carved inside holes – a thing of fantasy, a touch of luxury.

He came to them accompanied by his entourage, bearing soft ostrich feathers, a royal gift offered to the queen of the kingdom of mice.

They received him with the reception of kings and comrades.

And they prepared for him a private wing in the king's acts, a hole inlaid with carvings and ornaments that bewitches the mind.

King Auster stuck his head into the hole palace. The touches of beauty and luxury captivated him. He began to flap his wings in ecstasy and turn his head in all directions. Taken by the artworks and engravings and drawings, his legs danced in open air. His entourage around him watched and wished they were in his place. He could see what they could not see; his body was with them, and his head was in the world of fantasy.

King Auster returned to his kingdom strutting with the delights he had seen. The king of the mice sent with him his private builder to build for King Auster a luxurious palace for him to bask in, where he could rest his head from the travail of rule and the troubles of the kingdom and creatures' affairs.

Auster became absorbed in the distraction of palaces and started to spend his time in sticking his head into holes, and his kingdom followed him in this distraction which flowed like water flows in a brook; you could see the ostriches drunk with the splendor of the decorated palaces, their heads in the ground and their bodies flapping in the air.

Their muscles wilted from laziness, and their sizes and weights increased from vanity; in extravagant riches they basked and in diversion they played.

No one flew any longer, and this displeased the minister, so he seized an opportune moment of cheer and came close to the king and counseled him:

"Your Majesty King Auster, would Your Majesty grace us with a clarification of your noble ostrich logic? For you are an example to the people, and they imitate you and follow in your footsteps without thought.

- **Why don't we learn something by which to benefit our kingdom,** protecting it from the dangers that surround it from all sides, instead of learning something to distract ourselves with, which exposes us to perishment while our head is in the dirt?

- **What logic is there in living in a palace of delusion,** which barely fits our heads while our bodies are in the open? Why don't we dig a palace that suits our size, in which we can save ourselves from the might of predators?

- **What logic is there in sticking our heads in the sands,** fleeing from the responsibilities of rule and the kingdom, and the cares of wife and children and work and debts, and dreaming that our private problems will be solved on their own?

- **What logic is there in a large ostrich-bird like us living in a small mouse hole**, instead of flapping our wings and flying?"

And what about you, dear reader? Is there not someone amongst us who is like Auster?

Many of us are like King Auster.

- **Those in our orbit consider us kings; they imitate us without thinking and inherit from us the behaviors of success and failure and the logics of wealth and poverty.** The coward gives birth to failing and poor people, and the brave gives birth to successful and rich people, just as ostriches lay ostrich eggs.

- **His financial situation is in the worst condition, and you see him fleeing from his worries with a trip outside the country by going into debt, or a new car bought with tedious installments**; he enjoys it momentarily like someone drunk, until when its sweetness has gone and its intoxication has worn off, then the worry of its debt haunts him. So, he drives a vehicle that owns him not he it, a vehicle that enslaves him with its installments, as one who sticks his head into the dirt of the mire, and peers with his head every once in a while and says: When will this condition change?

- **He possesses wings of skills and abilities but does not take advantage of them and doesn't fly with them** to successes and a better life.

- **He spreads his feet to the size of his small blanket, instead of building a palace** fitted to his large size.

- **He sticks himself forcefully into a job smaller by far than the size of his qualifications or squeezes himself into a poor livelihood that does not meet his basic necessities**, reasoning that this is better than nothing, and that contentment is a treasure that is never exhausted, like an ostrich that covers its head, convincing itself that covering its head suffices it.

King Auster replied to him with verses from their holy book:

"Why should we fly, when our food is on the earth?

Better to walk, when we are so large in girth.

And if we fly, flying is not the danger worth.

And in the belly of the earth,

We feel enemies' vibrations, giving evils wide berth.

And our eggs we inspect from time to time, hiding them in our hearth."

King Auster recited them fluidly from memory without thinking, for they were holy verses engraved in the heart and mind.

The minister said, "My Lord, we can reduce our weight and strengthen our wings; we could build high walls or dig bigger holes, and we can take advantage of our large eyes and long necks to survey the enemies from afar. We can consult the most skilled experts; we have a national fortune in ostrich feathers and large eggs, and we can take advantage of our fortunes in manufactures and trade exchanges, and in attracting thinking minds to our nascent kingdom."

The king cried: "This is our religion and doctrine. Take warning, minister. This is our holy logic!"

Auster's Assassination

Years passed, and one day while the ostriches were obliviously unaware, a humongous hungry eagle circled over the ostrich kingdom, searching for a fat prey to sate its hunger, and Auster as was his habit was flapping rapturously with his head stuck in the palace, so the eagle descended upon Auster and securely planted its talons in his neck, callously and abruptly strangling him, killing him immediately.

Grief over the death of King Auster pervaded all areas of the kingdom, and a mourning period of three days was announced, then the kingdom pledged allegiance to his son the prince as a king by heredity.

The minister came with advice anew, in the presence of the elders and notables:

"Sire, do you not see what befell your martyr father?

The eagle did not let him be and killed him in an atrocious manner; it assassinated him while he stuck his head in the palace of the holes in safety. He died without any sense of pain or feeling, while everyone basked in their palaces of luxury, and they did not hear him calling, 'Save me! Save me!'

And today you, O prince, are the ruler of the kingdom, succeeding your martyr father; the matter is now in your hands and all eyes fall upon you.

Why does not our ostrich populace learn something other than sticking our heads into the sands?

What think you of learning to fly like the rest of the birds, and escaping from predators and immense dangers? And what think you…"

The assembly was enraged by the minister's daring and interrupted him

He is criticizing the martyr King Auster, founder of the ostrich state; this is an excursion from the holy ostrich logic and disbelief in the Clear Book, and a revolution against the inherited customs and followed traditions. We must set a limit for this absconding apostate!

And everyone cried in the face of the minister and recited with one voice:

Why should we fly when our food is on the earth?

"Better to walk when we are so large in girth.

And if we fly, flying is not the danger worth.

And in the belly of the earth,

We feel enemies' vibrations, giving evils wide berth.

And our eggs we inspect from time to time, hiding them in our hearth."

They recited it fluidly and with reverence.

Such is a Repressive Society.

Such is a repressive society; the people around you repress you and don't allow you to think or try. They memorize excuses and barriers that make change impossible; they parrot them, they reiterate them, they repeat them like a broken record. They pass them down by heredity generation after generation as if they were verses from a holy book, and they blast them in your face in one shot; they don't encourage you to venture outside the bounds of the box.

Where Are You, O Beheader?

They practice group terrorism on everyone who dares, so he surrenders and kneels, placing his head between the heads awaiting the beheader!

This is what King Auster did, and this is what ostriches still do, and this is the nature of the masses and the sleepers; they wait for death and the eagle's beheading attack.

The prince stood up and cried angrily:

"Silence!

What is this strange talk, O minister? I smell the scent of revolution and betrayal. This is the way of the ostriches and the way of my martyr father; he lived on it and on it he died. Are you an ostrich like us or what? This is open disbelief in our primordial ostrich logic and a downright call to revolution against the rule of our long lineage!"

"Your Majesty," said the minister, "pardon, my Lord. I am your obedient servant."

"I had heard you counseling my martyr founding father with this talk many years ago," said the prince. "My father replied to you with verses from our holy book, and even so you are still prattling on with your heresies, and here you are again repeating the same depravity today!"

"But Your Majesty, let me complete my point and present to Your Majesty my argument…"

"Hold your tongue. My father told you before, **"This is our religion and doctrine. Take warning, minister. This is our holy logic!"** It seems you will not be convinced unless we cut off your heretic head… **Guards!"**

"Mercy, my Lord," the minister pleaded. "Mercy, my Lord, mercy…"

Crazy Suicidal Logic

This is the logic of Auster and Auster's people; like most people, they have knowledge and diverge from it. They see the fatal result and don't repent. The writing is on the wall, but they don't see it. They have a strange indifference; they walk as agreed on one cipher, and a suicidal automatic unexplainable logical line, as if they had been created for hardship, or are being forced, their life decisions out of their hands, and their present and future out of their control.

Such is our disappointment.

We constantly excuse our disappointment with outside circumstantial excuses. We give them the status of a sacred god. We convince ourselves and chain our will to them, and we use them to defend our poverty, failure and cowardice; excuses that discourage us from trying and make change seem impossible. That is a false, wrongful god that shows you your cowardice as wisdom, your fear as caution, and your poverty as contentment!

The Logic of Poverty Spawns Poor People

We don't search for change because we fear ambiguity and risk-taking, and we lean toward the perceptible even if the perceptible is shaky and weak and incapable of supporting us. As such, we keep walking towards our demise with the staff of an incorrect and crooked logic.

You have become used to always creating excuses and justifications so that you can hang on them your miseries and poverty and failure:

- **My income is not enough.**

- **My work is hard.**

- **The market's down.**

- **The time isn't right.**

- **My wife spends too much money.**

- **The kids have a lot of requests.**

- **Circumstances aren't favorable.**

- **I am unlucky.**

- **My health is deteriorating.**

- **Everyone does it.**

- **No one's tried that.**

- **Why take a risk?**

- **A bird in the hand worth two in the bush.**

- **Once I turn forty.**

- **After my kids' engagement.**

And the list goes on…

Instead of making the impossible possible, we make the possible impossible!

Humans' behavior oftentimes contradicts reason, and reality proves that it's within our ability to forge logic and drive it to make the impossible possible. For the most part, however, we surrender to the power of logic, leaving it to forge us and drive us toward making the possible impossible.

Surrendering to the rule of logic loses us the freedom of choice.

When we let logic rule our lives, we lose our freedom of choice, and our control over our fate and present and future is shaken. At that point, we lose our confidence and become cowards.

Life does not submit to the fanciful laws of your head.

The existence of fanciful laws that explain matters does not make those matters logical; who said logic was an immutable law of physics?

Rather, logic is a custom we have become used to by seeing it repeated often, until it became a logic conceded to like an unbreakable fanciful law. **These fanciful laws that roost and breed in our heads are what rule us and direct us, but life does not recognize them and does not submit to them.**

For the most part, logic is nothing but a kind of comfortable delusion that we convinced ourselves of; we gave it the standing of scientific fact and proven law so that we can summon psychological reassurance and feel control.

Logic is a conclusion springing from what we see and are familiar with; it is not governed by a proven and specific law. And because humans don't like to live in dark environments that make them feel a loss of control and disturb their heartbeat, they continuously and with great effort seek desperately to discover the laws around them. Then when they fail to deduce a clear law, they resort to inventing a psychological imaginary law by which to ease their minds and return to them the delusion of control.

Logic is not a law but rather outside the law; it could be a fable or a crazy spell.

And such was the case of Auster's surrender…

He surrendered to the logic of cowardice and his descendants surrendered after him.

They surrendered to the logic of the ostriches; they latched onto the logic of poverty and weakness and need. They placed their heads in holes and laid their necks onto the guillotine of life, waiting for death to descend upon them suddenly like a hawk; they don't know when it will come to them or how or where. They lived as ostriches and died as ostriches and left behind ostriches!

Max's Adventures - The Disabled Mouse Flies

When "Max," the mouse without feathers, flies, then what kind of logic is that?

You could believe that a mouse has become a musician who could compete with the birds in singing; mice don't warble but they produce a sharp screeching sound, and it's not far-fetched that with some courage and training that the mouse could screech out a note, its screeches resembling the tunes of singing birds. As for a mouse flying, this is completely impossible in the conventions of logic!

Max, a Small Disabled Mouse

In contrast to Auster the great king, Max was a small, unique, orphaned, and disabled mouse. His mother claimed that he was the result of a biological mutation; she brought him out of her belly with the head of a mouse and fleshy appendages extending along the length of his sides and meeting at his hands and feet, in the shape of two wings of thin flesh.

Max was a foundling

Max was not actually a mutation as his mother circulated; Max was a foundling adopted by a mouse who could not give birth. She claimed after the death of her husband that Max was her newborn so that he could cheer her in her loneliness and give her the feeling of motherly affection, and so that he would not be expelled from the kingdom. She believed he was a disabled mouse and did not realize that he was the pup of a bat.

All the reasons for Max's failure were present and surrounded him from all sides.

He had lived the life of a toiling, disabled, poor, and orphaned mouse without a father. He was not able to run with his peers, dig with his claws, and would crawl on the ground with difficulty.

He lived a pariah and suffered much bitterness.

Max lived a pursued pariah. He suffered the youngsters' bullying; they would pull him along the ground, laughing as they pulled, causing him pain and injuries all over his scrawny body, as the skin on his fleshy appendages was thin and not covered by fur or hair. The mouse would rush to him with a mother's care to shoo away the troublemakers, weeping for her only child's condition, wiping his tears and licking his wounds as he wept with anguish and distress.

Max is Enraged

The bullying that Max suffered caused him to live resenting and raging against his society. He had an open and enlightened mindset that could not accept crooked logic and would not assent to bowing and surrendering to the pressure of society. He did not believe in assumptions, and this is what made him continuously search and dig for a way to get out of his predicament. His mother would not be there for him his whole life and he must work diligently and rely on himself.

And the chance arrived the day King Auster visited the mouse kingdom.

Max came close to Auster, that creature with wings and feathers, and his attention was caught by those wings on his back, so he asked him about the function of those wings. Auster replied scornfully, "Supposedly, I can fly with them," and began to cackle in derision at a disabled boy, and walked away arrogantly, grazing and enjoying riches.

Max returned to his mother and asked her about the meaning of flying.

She told him about a ferocious hawk. It had wings like Max's appendages, but they were covered in feathers; it would flap them then soar into the sky, and drop onto mice to catch them, and fly with them to his nest where he would devour them.

She spoke to him as she trembled with fear and warned him against approaching the hawk's nest that rested atop the high tree.

Brave Max's eyes lit up, and he determined to reach the hawk's nest no matter what price it cost him, but an airtight plan was necessary since he was disabled. And if the hawk saw him, his end was certain.

He contemplated and considered, and probed and pondered, then began to prepare to set off on the adventure.

He went to a nearby tree to practice climbing it, and quickly discovered his skill in climbing trees and grabbing onto branches. Then he began to suspend himself by his legs with his head hanging down, and he took to wrapping his wings like a cloak around his body and swinging like a tree leaf.

A Devilish Plan

A devilish plan sparked in his mind, and he decided at last to venture to the hawk's high tree.

Max crawled with his maximum speed to where the hawk's nest was so he could watch how it flew. He climbed the nest's tree, taking advantage of the camouflage skill he had gained; every time the hawk glimpsed his movement, he hung himself like a dry branch or a swinging tree lead, and thus he climbed and camouflaged until he got close enough to the hawk to watch its flight.

The hawk flew and Max's heart flew with delight, and his mouth dropped in astonishment from what he witnessed. He had seen a bird fly for the first time in his life, and the idea of flight occupied his heart and core. It was the only way that would let him overcome his disability, so he could live a dignified, free life, far from the life of poverty and weakness and need, awaiting pity and crumbs.

Max crawled down to the tree he had trained in, climbed to a safe height, took to flapping his wings and moving them until he felt the force of air striking them, and jumped. He soared a little and smacked into a rock, nearly breaking his bones on it.

He tried another time and a third and a fourth, until the sun set, and he returned home beat up.

His mother berated him and scolded him for his risk-taking, and she began to persuade him to stop his attempt, because what he was doing was insanity: the birds that could fly had a beak and tail and feathers. As for him, he was just a small, weak, and disabled mouse with appendages. Here was Auster: despite being a strong king and a large bird, he did not fly. And she warned him of the governor's force if he found out!

He nearly died!

He did not give up and was not deterred, and every day he would come back with bruises and contusions; until one day, the youngsters found him cast on a rock unconscious, and they wailed and carried him to his mother thinking he had died, but he quickly regained consciousness.

His Ordeal with Prison

The youngsters began to be affected by Max's story. He had told them about how he had tricked the hawk and seen its flight, and terror spread throughout the kingdom fearing for the youngsters from his insanity.

The king heard of Max's insanity and his new religion, and he sent the soldiers to bring Max to him in chains and iron.

The king spoke to him and became convinced of his disbelief and rebellion; how dare a poor disabled small orphan criticize the forefathers' logic and break the grandfathers' customs? Then imprisoning him and punishing him is a must!

Max lived in the prison chained in a solitary cell, and the worst colors of torture were practiced on him to bring him back to his religion and senses. And he spent the nights dreaming of flying, not caring for the whip marks that lined his delicate body.

And the commotion died down.

Everyone heard of Max's punishment; the youngsters were terrified, the adults were deterred, and the new religious commotion died down.

House Arrest

His mother visited him with a special royal permit; when she saw him in that condition, she took pity on him, and she pleaded with the king, begging him to release Max, as he was the only one after his father.

The king granted her request out of sympathy for her, after much insistence from her and vows. Her son would not leave the house or return to his disbelief, or else he would return to captivity and torture.

His body recovered and he returned to realize his dream.

Max rested some days until he had recovered and regained his strength, and the idea of flight tempted him anew, so he left the house through the backdoor when his mother was distracted. He crawled sneakily, hiding from the soldiers' eyes until he reached the tree. This time, he climbed to the top and decided to risk everything for the sake of his dream, for which he had sacrificed so much already.

A Mouse Realizes What Contradicts Logic and Opposes Reason

He gathered all his energy and courage, jumped from above, and took to flapping and flapping as he dropped plummeting toward the ground. He moved his wings in all directions, and it seemed as though he would inevitably smack into the ground and become pulverized. He consigned himself to God's keeping, closed his eyes, and flapped with his maximum strength and energy.

And a moment before he touched the ground, he flew. He shouted with joy, not believing he had survived and flown at last. He called to the small mice, and his mother rushed out to the sound of his shouting. She wept when she saw her disabled son realizing his impossible dream and doing what was against logic and contrary to reason.

The Logic of the Brave Versus the Logic of the Coward

- Little **Max** did not accept living in a hole that fit him and his family. Large **Auster** lived in a hole that only fit his head.

- **Max** lived as a mouse, but he refused the life of mice. **Auster** lived an ostrich, but he accepted the life of mice.

- **Max** is a mouse without a beak or tail or feathers, yet he flew. **Auster** is a bird with a beak and tail and feathers, yet he did not attempt flight.

- **Max** lived in poverty and was disabled but he did not surrender to his fate. **Auster** lived rich and whole, but he surrendered to his logic.

- **Max** the small defied his disability and plunged into dangers that nearly cost him his life, and he lived on a dream by which he could prove himself. **Auster** the large lived comfortably rich, lost in intoxication, grazing with the slackers without a destination or goal.

- **Max** freed himself from the power of the logic of mice and bridled it. **Auster** was controlled by the logic of ostriches and was dominated by it.

- **Max** defied society, the king, the soldiers, and the prison cell. He did not relinquish his dream and did not bury himself alive. **Auster** was the king and held the power and authority, but he buried his head in a hole whilst alive.

Max the Brave adopted the Logic of Wealth, and Auster the Coward adopted the Logic of Poverty

A Scientific Logic: Are Humans Predestined or Free-Willed?

The laws of physics can be applied to the material principles of the universe but not to the spiritual lives of humans. Science, reality, and observations prove that you were not created according to a rational, scientific, solid, and proven law; this brings you outside the scientific laws that steer the universe, as the origin of your creation violates the principles of science and blasts away the laws completely, so the soldiers of science stand helpless in front of the realization of the essence of the soul and life.

This is what has confounded scientists and driven them crazy, because they are programmed to mold nature to a clear rational law of the universe. The power of scientists wanes and vanishes without the laws of science, because the absence of laws strips them of their medallions and distinguishments in the field of beliefs, which is full of miracles that break scientific logic and Intangibles that exceed the power of the mind to picture.

And this is what led some of them to invent the theories of creational chaos and chance and random mutations so they can explain their own creation and the beginning of their lives, and they gave them the standing of proven scientific fact even though they possibly violate the laws to begin with and might even blow away scientific foundations entirely.

The scientifically proven.

Without going into what scientists are still trying to grasp in the dark since the beginning of time, what is certain is that you were created with your spiritual and bodily composition in a way that breaks established laws and scatters every solid scientific logic. This means that no steering law to govern you can be applied to your very existence in this composition, and no scientific facts that mold you can control it.

You are given choice with all certainty.

You are a creature with free will in the midst of this organized world, after all. No law to chain you can be applied to your existence nor any fact to steer and capture you; it is for you to pick what logics and hypotheses as the tool of your mighty mind leads you to.

Be Heretical to be Free

And so that your choice can be successful, you must free yourself from the captivity of the familiar and the inherited that chains your giant mind, which no artificial computer can match. This will not happen except through heresy which does not accept crooked logic and does not believe in irrational myths nor in spells that make you hallucinate in broad daylight!

Your brain has begun to fry for sure.

Your brain has begun to fry for sure after we have nearly pulled out the horns with which logic forcefully and fiercely rams. Your logic that you have left to nest in your head and nourished its horns and developed them, here now rises up to obstruct our campaign, opposing the solution of the behavioral complex that chains your launch. We are close to breaking those horns!

A Cipher Break

I nearly killed my brother by using the destructive weapon of ciphers.

Catch your breath now. It's necessary to take a short and dangerous training break in one of the oases of youth before we launch our last obliterating campaign!

How ugly I was when I exploited my caring brother's cipher and nearly killed him; we had come to blows that day on the front terrace of our house. He was and still is stronger than me. I cried cast on the ground as he regarded me. My eyes were overflowing with tears.

The First Time I Died

I was laying on my right side, and then focused my overflowing eyes on his eyes. I abruptly stopped crying, breathing, and moving, and did not blink. My brother stared at me astonished; this was the first time I died!

He nearly died from the severity of fear and shock; he went running terrified to my mother and she followed him in fear for him. I did not expect the force of his caring and sensitivity to that dangerous degree, even though it was he who had saved me from the wasps' nest, and it was he who returned and sacrificed himself for my sake, and all his concern was to save my life!

He reached my mother and he had lost the power to speak. My mother was terrified by the hue of his color, and she started to calm some of his fear and terror. Then, when he saw me alive, he spoke, and my mother berated me with severity and astonishment, saying, **"Do you want to kill your brother, you sad soul?"**

Even though he was the one who hit me and was older and more muscular than me, I nearly killed him without the slightest movement, blink, or even breath!

The weapon of ciphers is a non-traditional weapon that could be exploited in a frightful and awful manner.

Genesis and Advancement in the Human Logic

Despite the mighty mind mechanisms that humans possess, their fear of the unknown and instinctive continuous seeking toward security and peace, after they had not found immovable life laws to make them feel consistency and stability, have made them resort to the delusion of logic in order to control their life and manage it; a logic that they have given the place of sacred law and let it govern and delimit the shape of their life and its paths.

They are only hypotheses and delusions that society fabulously invented so that life can appear to be stable and comprehensible.

Is a poor person born poor and a rich person born rich?

Logic is the result of environmental and societal experiences; it acts as a fertile topic in the study of human societal behaviors in terms of how the logic of human societies is affected by the inference environment and life climate.

The poor draw their logic from the conventions of poverty that stem from an ungrateful, complaining, cowardly, surrendering environment; and the rich draw their logic from the conventions of wealth that stem from an optimistic, adventurous, courageous, and defiant environment.

Therefore, the poor lives by the logic of the poor and gains poverty and misery, and the rich lives by the logic of the rich and gains wealth and comfort.

Hang It on Fate

The one who bemoans his luck because they were born poor to stay poor, while there is one who was born with a golden spoon to keep the golden spoon in his mouth. They stone fate with what is not in it and hang the causes of their misfortunes on external circumstances, running away from the responsibility that requires them to take new paths they are not familiar with and obligates them to rebel against a jailer who fetters them with the delusions of an erroneous logic.

All of this goes back to the ignorance about the chemistry of the logic that they have left for years to weave prison cells out of the threads of delusion that chain them and prevent their rebellion against insubstantial spider silk… **The human being is that coward!**

"I disbelieved early and lived a rebellious heretic!"

The misfortunes of the man in the cell and the events in the adventures of Auster and Max are continuously repeated in my reality and yours without us feeling. I also had to rebel at an early age like Max, or else I would have faced Auster's fate and lived the misfortunes of the mouse man.

If I had not become a heretic at a young age, my book would not have reached you. The Arabic language teachers at my school were not pleased with my pen; they tried all forms of repression to silence my gift of rhetoric, but I refused. Then I saw in front of me a road that the masses of people took, so I turned away from it and betook myself to an abandoned road and walked.

They considered my runaway writings to be rhyming mouse squeals, impudence against the religion of poets. They considered my heretic style to be rudeness destructive to the thresholds of literature and outside the conventions of the guardians, like an annoying cricket on the drapes of their sacred Kaaba.

And even now you'll find those who ask, and you might also ask:

How can an economist CPA and Arab living in Israel write prose and poetry and literature and philosophy?

And this is what had chained me until I realized the secret cipher that set me free. I crushed the idols of logic and set off with this book of mine that is in your hands!

Are Humans Apes?

On the one hand, a logic that tells you about creatures changing their shapes and bodies, and that believes in their evolution in a way that lets them grow wings and limbs, and that humans are nothing but talking apes with a tongue that has evolved over the ages.

And on the other hand, a logic that says that between apes and humans is a vast difference and a quantum leap that no human mind can comprehend, no scientific law can cover, and no ideological logic can encompass, as humans' leap is a revolutionary psychological one, not a physical ornamental leap.

As an economist, I lean toward practical ideas, as this is not a book of religious doctrine to go into these unknowns; this is a comprehensive behavioral and developmental doctrine book, and when science proves in some of its excavations that some creatures perhaps evolved their bodies, even if by mutation, and in an essential or nonessential manner, then it's worthier for behaviors and instincts to evolve!

So, don't be more cowardly than circus animals.

I won't tell you that there are creatures that have evolved their biological bodies over the ages so they can adapt and survive as they say, but I refer you to take a look at circus animals.

Look at how they've been trained on amazing movements and acrobatics that astonish the mind. They have changed their ways and behaviors, even though they are dominated by an instinctive logic that firmly chains them and stupidly so, because they don't have minds to free them from the slavery of instinct.

What's more striking is that you find humans amongst us who are incapable of changing their ways, despite the giant minds they carry over their heads!

Renounce Every Logic That Chains You

I would really have been a victim to a repressive educational system. At home, school, university, and in the job market and business world, you must forge your own path, swimming against the current of the illogical, or else you will be part of the sweeping current of routine and a clone of what they wanted for you. Your skin color, fingerprint, and height of stature are not what define who you are, and you shouldn't let them limit and define you; your reactions and steps are what lead you to where you are now and where you will be after now. **The same steps will lead to the same results… so renounce every logic that chains you!**

Repressive School Systems

My whole life I would write essays and get heaps of compliments and praise, until I met a teacher whom even the wildest wonders or hardest labors would not please; he would not give me a grade higher than 80%, and I would always curse under my breath.

I would read the scribbles of a classmate who had just received 95%, and my inner voice would explode—"For God's sake, how come?"

Then I advanced a grade, and we had an instructor of the same sort as the first – rather, harsher and even worse than him – so I wept over my first teacher, and I insisted on my illogical style of writing, despite its flavor not pleasing my teacher and not suiting his inherited literary logic.

I Don't Want to Be a Fashion Model

There are teachers who want you to write in their traditional way — introduction, body, and conclusion — a planned and predetermined routine writing, just like a model's performance on the catwalk. They don't want you to chirp outside the flock of the mapped-out logic even if that logic is infidel. **They are repressive teachers who want you to be a copy of the book of Al-Jahiz, timeworn and obsolete.**

I'm not discounting literature and writers nor teachers and principals, because they are also victims of society and susceptible to the creep of an incorrect and imprisoning logic which could block them from seeing matters outside the perspective of the idol of logic that they worship.

A Highly Esteemed Teacher

And then we had a poet- and doctor-teacher. A professor, not a dictator, and that was in the beginning of twelfth grade – that is, in the last stretch of school. He did me justice from the first piece of writing, and, driven by his strong admiration in my writing, he stood me in front of the students to read it aloud.

Ah… for the first time in three barren years! He even noted in the footer of the page and signed it, **"A topic worthy to be published and in it is a moral for those who care to listen"** dated 15/9/1993.

His praise was repeated, and he injected into my writings a confidence that accompanied me more than a quarter of a century. He was a poet and a creative; my creative writings and unconventional opinions did not frighten him, and he encouraged me to the fullest, despite the heated discussions and sharp tone that used to boil up between us as a serious and sharp-tongued teenager, and he would accept my sharpness with his wide smile and loud laugh.

The Logic of "I"

In our traditional schools, we've gotten used to every question having only a single correct answer, and that's the answer the teacher wants to hear, even though life often does not have a single solution. If it did, we would have continued to light fire with stones, and I don't know what I would be wearing now, I wonder – it's better if we don't go too far.

Through this way, all these generations and societies ruled by **"the logic of I"** have been generated, **and it is a fierce logic that takes control of its owner and drives them rabid; it's akin to a mad dog that rules its owner and seeks to impose its control and dominance over the logic of other people through any means. It does not discuss, listen, understand, change, adjust, or yield; it imposes the solution to problems by force with the logic of muscles and strong-arming.**

The management of the world, societies, economies, and relationships requires someone who has a flexible leadership logic, who accepts criticism and discussion and improvement. They don't sanctify logic and don't let it control their behaviors and reactions, and they don't give it the standing of indisputable scientific fact.

An Appeal from A Rebellious Student, To the Teacher Ruled By the Logic of "I"

Why the teacher specifically?

Because they're instructors, educators, and role models…

Because they're either the best heroes or the worst criminals.

Dear repressive teacher:

- My rebellion will not die down with the cannon of chastisement, and regardless of whether my answer is correct, it is not your right to point the gun of your cane in my face, and it is not at all your right to encourage my classmates to interrupt me, just because I honestly said my opinion and so gave an answer that did not fit your whim. **By this way, you fashion the next dictator from a small child.**

- You want me to be a carbon copy of you and your ideas, **and I want to be me as I am**, free, loose, and rebellious against selfishness and your logic of "I"

- Why do you want me to silence myself and cower, and place my head under the guillotine of society, so that the students in the class will grant me affection, amity, and love? **This is collective rape.**

- Why don't you want me to keep my personal answer and reveal it, and defend it without losing your respect and the respect of my peers? **This is exactly extortion.**

- **I won't allow your incorrect logic to straddle me, like it has straddled you, with the whip of menaces and threats that were practiced on you in your childhood, and I won't allow your wild logic to kill the young creative inside me, and I won't permit it to gag the horse of brave leadership logic that I have straddled.**

- **I demand that you to direct the students of your class to accept me as I am**, with the color of my eyes and skin and with my thoughts and religion and race; **have you forgotten your educational role in the areas of the Exodus?**

I Boldly Rebelled Against the Injustice of my Hebrew Language Teacher

Yes, I rebelled because I don't accept injustice even if by a single point. He was a temporary substitute teacher, and I protested that my grade should be 100% and not 99%. I showed him that my answer was correct and not his, but he refused to correct my paper and adjust my grade. The logic of arrogance and the logic of "I" took over him, and the logic of vengeance and stubbornness took over me. I was no longer that young boy whose cheeks could be slapped, and his mettle broken trivially and contemptibly while escaping the consequences of that action. I exhausted him with desperate discussion and insistence, and he was only saved by the bell ringing.

I did not give up!

I waited for the next period to start. I left my class and went directly to an adjacent classroom that he was teaching in. I knocked on the door, and when he opened it, he was surprised and annoyed by the extent of my rudeness. **He closed the door in my face** and continued teaching.

I knocked a second time; he cried out as he opened the door violently, biting his lip threateningly, and I told him **"Give me my point."** He re-entered grumbling angrily in front of the students of his class.

I knocked a third time and heard him burst out in the classroom: he hit the board with his hand; his chair screeched sharply as it was pushed back, scraping on the floor and slamming into a wall; he threw his chalk at the door, and it crumbled like an exploding bullet; and he came toward me like a rampaging bull, so I told him with provocative calmness, **"Even if you were to pop a vein, I won't relinquish my right"**!

No One Understood the Secret

Neither the Hebrew language teacher nor the students in my class and the adjacent class understood the secret of my stubborn insistence in this insensitive fashion, and for the sake of one point.

As for me, this point was what separated injustice from justice, and a matter of principle that was impossible for me to yield on in any case, so I left him and complained about him to the homeroom teacher, who wiped the grade and changed it to 100% and told me to forget about him.

Didn't I tell you that life slowly prepares us for coming opportunities?

This incident accompanied me to my university with the criminal jurisprudence lecturer that I spoke to you about, and it was the beatings and injustice that happened to me in my childhood that fueled and motivated me to provoke some of the professors and lecturers for an old grudge I had not forgotten, and for my logic of rebellion against injustice no matter how slight or small the size of the injustice is, and no matter who may be its doer.

A Rebellious Appeal to the Repressed and Oppressed of the Free World

Dear "repressed", dear "oppressed", and those unaware that they're repressed and oppressed!

No matter how much you rise or fall, and even if you were the president of the greatest empire in the world, you're a victim, and your condition is miserable, whether in the apparent or the hidden; perhaps the perpetrator is a harsh father or stepfather, or a severe mother or stepmother, or an abusive husband or wife, or a repressive teacher or lecturer, or school or university bullies, or an exploitative company manager or work colleagues, or a blackmailing worker or employee, or a brand or drug giant, or a despotic state president or government, or a brutal diplomatic equal or national traitor, or a prosperous but ungracious giver or an ungrateful indigent...

The perpetrators are many, the victims are in the millions, whether aware or not.

The time has come for you to escape from and discard the role of the victim.

The time has come for you to escape from and discard the doctrine of cowardice.

The time has come for you to escape from and discard the deification of circumstances.

The time has come for you to escape from and discard surrendering to reality.

The time has come for you to escape from and discard the torture of oppression and the pain of repression.

The time has come to renounce the divinity of the logic that chains you, and rebel against the whip that rules you. Break the horns of holy things and halos that enslave you; you were born free and dignified so don't let any human being repress you.

Breathe out…

Your heartbeat is speeding up now.

Take a deep breath…

You are not alone; I'm still here with you

And I won't leave you hanging in the air like this

Don't follow me…

But accompany me to the end

Because I'm exactly like you

And I'll stay with you

On your side and next to you.

Right now, you're in a boiling and enraged state, and a field trip is necessary in which we plunge into bewitching adventures.

Right now, you're in need of a relaxing trip, to cool down the fires of your rage little by little – a hunting trip to internalize the meanings and study the world of the seas, in order to get to know the human fish and the ways of seafaring. You will return from the trip with a fishing pole and net in your quiver with which to hunt your fate and record your future.

Let's plunge into bewitching trips and practical applications that will rest you and calm your terror and nerves; they will help you to log your personal book and understand your obscure cipher.

ACT

BEWITCHING IMPLEMENTATIONS

The Arena of Logics - A Fight to the Death

In one minute, approximately 265 enter it while 110 leave it.

The number of incorrect logics in the world is impossible to count, just as it is impossible to count the human souls that are born and waste away. The global net population increase is more than 220 thousand lives in one day; that is, the number of births exceeds the number of deaths by approximately 155 lives in one minute. Each life is a world unto its own. **You don't know which of these lives is the life of war or the life of peace that was presented to the world or left it.**

A Hushing Humanitarian Stand

We cannot bypass statistical numbers without a humanitarian stand. In 2018, 2.5 million children in the first month of their lives left the arena, a third of whom left very early on the first day they arrived in this world, and most of them died from preventable causes… **where is the humanitarian logic?**

Logic is a War Machine That Destroys the World

Don't take the power of logic lightly. Its effects are not just on the areas of your personal life, but also on world peace. Behind the world wars and Middle Eastern conflicts, and the internal struggles in America and China and Europe and world countries, is an arrogant logic.

A Universal War Impossible to Contain

It is impossible to find a problem in any spot in the universe, on Earth or outside of it, among humans or non-humans, without the "logic of I" behind it. **Even our father Adam's first sin was caused by a Satanic selfish logic!**

The wrong logic costs its owner and the entire universe woes which the world pays for; Satan dragged his descendants and humanity into an eternal struggle and endless woes, its effects transcending the bounds of heaven and time. **The effects of wrong logic could reach beyond their owner to reflexive circles of family, society, nation, and the world, which may not be possible to contain at all.**

Don't Fall for the Neckties.

Follow the struggles of the world around you. Political discussions and international summits and intercessions and conferences of war and peace, all of them in neckties. Even if you were to dive deeply into the worst thorny issues, you would find that their solution in all certainty did not need to reach these levels of world tensions which brought about disasters and woes and sped up the rhythm of weaponization and greed for the development of tools for quick and complete destruction.

For God's Sake, Tell me.

How is two children fighting in the neighborhood or at school, or two rogues stabbing each other or exchanging shots, different from the international war of armies and militias?

Only one thing is different: the necktie and the tools.

The struggles are fiercer and more dangerous as humans get older a generation and go higher in status and increase in elegance.

Life proves that masks and costumes and veneers and positions don't change the nature of scoundrels and hooligans. Life lessons confirm, and the reasonable logic establishes, and this Act will uncover, some of the sorceries that you used to be ignorant of.

A pivotal practical summary:

Don't regard the small events of your life as childhood leisure memories; they are the mirror of your future and a microcosm of your life path. Rather, childhood is the true picture of life without neckties or makeup. Each experience is a brick that polishes your logic and develops your personality; either you lead it to where you want to get to, or you surrender to it wherever it takes you.

The Story of the Day My Grandfather's Den Betrayed Me

The Life of a Neurotic Child... Everything Has a Price

How hard it is to live a rebel from a young age. After the incident in sixth grade that I mentioned before and which changed the course of my life and what I cared for, I devoted myself to my studies and began to distance myself from the hooligans, and as a result, they attributed to me the epithet "neurotic." I hated being called by that loathsome name, and I faced bullying at times during which I feared for myself from the boys in our neighborhood and the students at the neighboring school, and I would run all the way home as they chased me with insults and threats and stones.

Accepting the role of the victim is giving up.

I did not accept the role of the victim and I did not stand watching. I met insults with insults and chasing with racing away and stone with stone and disbelief with disbelief – it happened that one of them blasphemed against my God, so I blasphemed against his God automatically without thinking, relying in all of this on my skills of comeback in karate and soccer.

Sport and play are the best educational life lessons.

Sports granted me astonishing tactical weapons which saved me from huge predicaments, just as they dragged me into dangers and challenges, some of which I didn't need.

Karate did not make me into Bruce Lee, as my build was thin like a scarecrow, and my grip was small and had no use against the swarthy boy of towering height who was the chief troublemaker in our neighborhood, nor against the giant blond of the neighboring school who forced his dominion over his young followers; they're my friends today and they will laugh a lot when they read my book. These events were the strongest developmental lessons I took in my life.

We did not have a VCR in our house and I had not heard of the cinema, but I acted in reality the hero of thriller and action films through the excitements I lived on the streets of my town while I was being chased.

Self-confidence is your most important weapon.

Karate gave me self-confidence and lightness of movement, and soccer gained me physical fitness. I was not the fastest one in running away but I had the most endurance. No one could pin me down or corner me. Catching me was impossible because I was very slippery and quick to dodge like a smooth hold; I could take off my shirt in a flash if needed, surprise with a punch or scratch in a glance, and kick with skill in the most sensitive areas without hesitation.

A delicate sense of security… activate your survival instinct!

A delicate sense of security was spawned in me with the experiences, and a stubborn survival instinct and notable reflexes as well. I mimicked monkey jumps, passing my time bouncing on the walls and atop the fig and walnut and chinaberry trees in the yard of our house, until I became skilled in climbing trees and walls. The young predators would damn me after every escape, and in one of their rhyming songs – I remember it as if it were today – they chanted in a unified tone and with one angry voice:

Damn your father… who raised you… in Baqa[5]

Escaping triumphant… Know how to escape.

As for me, I stood with my heart beating next to the green gate of my grandfather's house, at the top of a rising road, panting safely, looking at them while they were at the bottom of the slope before I entered my grandfather's den, but not before I threw my stone at them and hurled childish

---

5   In Arabic, "yel'aan abaka… allathi rabbaka… fi Baqa."

provocations at them to rile them and avenge myself. I was not completely innocent. **I would do this daily then enter the courtyard of my house triumphant despite running away and brimming with the euphoria of escape.**

Surrendering to the reality of life is the easiest of ways.

I could have announced my subordination to the head of the gang and enter safely into his protection, but I became addicted to the adrenaline of rebellion that cost me psychological effort and unusual preparations for a child of my age; I could not leave the house safely unless I was accompanied by my older brother or one of my cousins.

Leaving the house alone required complicated safety precautions, in case I met a group of my victims whose chief had spilled my blood, especially those fast ones that could surround you by surprise in their area of control and catch you off guard and unaware. I had to avoid the houses of some of the youngsters or the alleys with dead ends.

Human childhood is a real, bare, picture of the lives of adults.

The human childhood was not a nurturing period that quickly came to an end, because the films followed me with human adults in the cells of life, and with some of the criminal jailers in the clothes of a teacher. The thriller and suspense films that I had mastered with children turned into tragedy horror movies with adults in the large jail of school, where they chain you in a cage governed by rules and protocols; where the tactics of karate don't work and there is no escaping the jailer's grasp.

And I have a very miserable memory with such a predator, when I stood next to my grandfather's den about to take revenge on her, as I had gotten used to time and again in my neighborhood heroics with the young predators…

Society could push toward crime at an early age!

I became determined to commit a crime with which to put out the child's wrath inside me. That day, my brother came running, panting and blowing alarm whistles: "Your teacher is in the neighborhood driving her car." I was in second grade at the time, and she was a temporary teacher subbing in for the main teacher on maternity leave.

I did not run away as was my habit… Life coerces us to do things we might not want!

Until that moment, whenever I heard that a teacher was nearby, I would flee the place because I was very shy, despite my fierceness. No one knew what my writhing insides hid; everyone expected me to run away as was my habit, except this time I did not.

Adults Are More Vicious Than Children, Even If It Is a Cultured and Elegant Lady

Just one day prior, she had practiced the arts of kung fu on my thin cheeks, and though it was not the first time it had happened, it was the most atrocious confrontation with a predator that smashed my face with her elegant palms, and I still remember the polish on her claws and the red of her lips as she bared her fangs, slapping me until the poor woman's strength collapsed; my evil cheeks hurt her hands. It was my first experience with feminine kung fu in an unequal and one-sided battle. **Did I not tell you that costumes and veneers don't change the nature of hooligans?**

Children Have Dignity… The Moment for Vengeance Arrives

Here comes the moment for vengeance from a vicious woman. Her fate led her to a territory governed by my rules. I stepped out of the den that had long stood by my side as I eyed the youngsters and provoked them at the boundaries of my kingdom, picked up a huge stone, and waited for the car to pass so I could throw the stone at it to smash it along with the woman inside it. My sense of security directed me to hide behind the wall of my grandfather's house, lurking and sneaking glances from behind the electricity pole until the moment of assault arrived. **I glimpsed her approaching the ambush and steadied my grip in readiness to shoot…**

And the moment of attack arrived!

My heartbeats sped up, sweat poured from my brow, worry about the consequences jumped to discourage me until fear took over me, and the forces of good wrestled with me until they won over me…

My grandfather's den betrayed me.

The stone fell from my hand without resistance. I stood nailed in place, stunned for moments that felt like hours. I was a coward for the first time and at the door of my house… I had been vanquished in the core of my kingdom. My grandfather's den had betrayed me.

A Pitiful Child?

Whoever finds out about some of the sides of my childhood will suppose conclusively that I was a pitiful child, but after I grew up, I discovered that our childhoods, no matter how callous or unjust their events seem to be, polish us and grant us life experiences that prepare us for the tumultuous real life.

The real failure is the fear of failure!

Wading into dangers is not dangerous. What's dangerous is that fear will prevent you from wading into those dangers. Most people fail in their lives because of the fear of failure. They refrain from realizing their aspirations and give up their dreams for fear of trying.

Don't stand still like a statue, and don't fear the might of ghosts.

Leadership requires going into an unaccustomed experience and taking a path that perhaps no one has embarked on before you. The one who fears darkness will dread walking in the labyrinths of life searching for successes, which await him there in a nearby corner that might be dark, or for a treasure set aside in abandoned environs!

All you have to do is overcome your fear; don't stand still like a statue. Move your hand toward the ignition button and turn on the headlamps so you can see the chance at your hand's reach. Some people have reached such degrees of cowardice that they dread turning on the light for fear of the might of ghosts.

Life examples from the reality of adults:

- **They dread leaving a miserable job** because they fear going into a more miserable experience!

- **They leave a profitable deal or let go of the opportune chance of a lifetime** fearing a loss or a gloat.

- **They dread changing their university major or studying another topic they love** fearing others' reaction over what they consider a failure and an affront.

I Helped Him Leave His University Studies

An extremely smart young man grudgingly joined the college of computer engineering to please his father. Studying turned into a nightmare for this young man; he was not able to study from the severity of his depression, and transferred from the southern Ben-Gurion University of Beersheba to the northern University of Haifa so he could change the depressive environment that had stuck to him. The young man suffered indescribably as he endured to please his father. His interest and gift were in another field.

I interceded with the young man's father. The father lost his mind when he found out about his son's intent to leave his studies. His concern was what people would say more so than his concern for his son. And after much effort to persuade him, the father softened finally and was convinced that his wrong logic was leading his son to certain failure, **and that winning his son and losing people's words was better than winning people's words and losing his son.**

And the young man studied the topic which he yearned for. He excelled in it to the utmost, and today he has become the pride of his father and family.

- **They don't part with a failed love story** and continue in the engagement until they get married and have children. They live hanging their marital life's failure on their victimized children and poor spouse, in a house haunted by hell where their return is hated.

They feared from the beginning to go into a new love experience, and they abandoned themselves to delusions and wishes. They thought the problems would be solved on their own after marriage or perhaps after having children, and they're still waiting for a miracle that will never happen.

I Was the Reason for a Couple's Divorce

I caused the separation of a young man engaged to a young woman. The young man and woman were from respectable families but joining between the engaged couple was impossible. All the paths of compatibility were blocked. There was not a single glimmer of hope for their marital success.

The families pressured them with full force to finalize the marriage, as each side saw the other side as an irrecoverable "catch." The families were possessed by an incorrect logic to begin with, because the ones who would be getting married were the two young people and not the two families, and separation does not mar modesty nor is it the end of the world. All the indications of failure predicted a certain divorce, not just between the couple themselves but rather a divorce between two families.

I stepped in and went ahead with the separation proceedings. It was not easy, and the matter was extremely embarrassing, especially after an engagement that had lasted two years and postponing the wedding several times. **I had undertaken a brave deed against a disastrous logic before the axe fell**, before the wedding ceremony and before there were victims and losses – children and alimony and courts and a wide familial dispute.

Shortly after, the young woman was married and had children, and neither her life nor his ended despite the separation.

Be brave and withdraw at the right time!

The First Killer

Fear is undoubtedly the first killer of successes, and it is undoubtedly the capital of a failing person.

There are those who have found a devilish way to exploit the logic of human fear through the depletion of humanity's wealth, and at the cost of people's sweat and fatigue and blood and nerves.

Insurance companies:

Insurance companies are built on the fear factor first and foremost, and their profits are directly proportional to its rise in frequency; today there is an official economic measure of the size of human and market fears.

They convince you that you are on the verge of having a car crash at every moment; you will be exposed to a workplace accident tomorrow; you will contract an incurable disease the day after tomorrow; your commercial warehouses will burn tonight; your house will have a short-circuit or be struck by lightning; a devastating earthquake is only a matter of time; the day you leave the country bad luck will accompany you on your trip; you might die at any moment and insuring your life is a must, as well as insurance for your profession, and insurance for your employees, and insurance for the managers… There isn't a thing left that they haven't created a special insurance policy for. **Have you heard of insurance for the left pinky or the right-hand ring finger?** A driver drives his car with complete confidence and he's happy, and suddenly remembers that his car insurance expired a month ago. During that same month he drove his car safe and confident, and as soon as he realizes, his balance is thrown off and his confidence is shaken. **He might be more concerned about his car insurance than about his car, and he might fear for the life insurance more than for his own life!**

Weapons manufacturers:

They develop an offensive weapon every day followed then by a defensive weapon, and they develop another offensive weapon followed then by another defensive one, and so on. They manufacture and produce and develop weapons for offense and defense, without any war or need looming on the horizon, and the people groan under the burden of debts and exorbitant taxes while they're submissive and silent.

A Button of Destruction and a Tweet for Reparation

And in the midst of the clamor of the feverish race, igniting wars becomes a logical and necessary thing from which there is no escape, as war is a necessity for making fear logical and exploitation reasonable, and if war does not start by itself you will find someone who will stir up disputes and ignite battles and purposefully contrive wars.

These are companies whose fuel is blood. They profit billions and zillions by igniting wars and inciting between nations and peoples. They intervene with the excuse of bringing peace but in reality, they intervene to prolong the war and stoke its lit wick. Wherever they intervene, notice how the issues have become complicated and violence widespread and reconciliation a complete impossibility.

And you'll find those who defend spilling the blood of innocents and cutting their limbs with the excuse of unavoidable necessity, to save humanity from an imminent danger or gloomy fate or terrorism about to happen… **and how ugly humans are when they obliterate thousands of innocents then tweet from the electronic above apologizing for wasting lives by mistake!**

Politicians:

They are the smartest and worst people in the exploitation of human logic. There are no ethics in modern politics; the political arena is without laws or regulations. When the seat of decision-making, personal interests, factional desires and partisan agendas are a higher national goal and loftier public aim, means become justified and wars a divine code that they evince with holy texts which they invoke on the masses and trample when alone. They exploit the scarecrow of fear and wave around the bloody shirt of war to win their political battles.

Automatically, politicians are susceptible to exploitation by companies and those who fund their parties and campaigns. They become obedient tools in hidden hands that move them. Politicians, in their turn, move the simple naive people, who rebel from time to time but how quickly they die down and surrender to their dim-witted logic!

"I learned lessons in 1999 that I will never forget: Despite the complicated circumstances and despite your need and lack, know your own worth and demand what you deserve!"

There is Nothing Like a Painful Experience

No matter how much people talk to you and advise you, nothing will convince you like a painful real event. It happened to me personally in 1999; I have told you that what you don't learn easily and readily, you will learn by the cane of pain and blows of tears.

You've shortchanged yourself before they shortchanged you.

Many people accept the lowest prices in return for their work and wares, and they don't demand their dues for fear of being fired or of a reaction whose consequences they cannot bear.

And this goes back to cowardice and fear of the unknown; they fear riding a new wave they have not tried before, and this is what makes their life a passive routine with no incentives or motivations. Leadership thinking requires from you daring, firmness, self-confidence, and self-evaluation of your real worth. **Cowards do not give themselves any worth or weight, and this is what makes them susceptible to exploitation and an easy meal for the greedy.** No one can ride you unless you bow your back and show your need and weakness.

I searched for Layla, but a landmine blew up in my face.

Like one who flies madly to Layla[6], in 1999 – my fourth year in university – I rushed eagerly to the vacancies board hanging in the front hall of the Hebrew University of Jerusalem, combing for a new advertisement from a distinguished account audit network, hoping to get an internship lasting two years, as it was a condition for professional certification required by the Board of Certified Public Accountants.

I did not need to reach the board to notice the new advertisements. I had memorized it by heart, and every

---

6   *"Majnun Layla* or *Layla's Mad Lover* is a famous 7th-century Arabic narrative poem.

change that occurred on it my heart would flutter for it from afar, just like lovers' hearts flutter unperturbed by distance.

Repeated Frustration

Frustration overwhelmed me each time I was refused, but how quickly my eagerness flamed up each time I sent my CV to a new office. I was living in a rosy dream as far as can be from the reality that I had imagined my whole life, as my father had painted for me. Jobs rushed to Jewish colleagues and offers were heaped on them, and I found myself panting fruitlessly after some offer… there was something wrong in the matter that bewildered me!

An Obscure Riddle

For weeks I made the pilgrimage to my hanging Mecca and prayed on my way. An unfair matter targeted me; my intelligence had not yet until that moment helped me to uncover the secret behind this failure. My university grades were through the roof, and I had a certificate of excellence upon which I was hired as a teaching aide with an outstanding CV; offers were supposed to have poured down on my lap like the torrential rains in the peak of winter, but there were only summer clouds that dried the mouth.

The Moment of Succor

One morning, I turned my face toward my hanging Mecca, the Mecca that I no longer prayed to as I used to do before, and that I no longer gazed at from afar. I walked toward it, my steps growing heavier by the minute, not caring for what awaited me; it had been two weeks since anything had changed on the board hanging on the wall…

What wretchedness, nothing new today either, how depressing it is! And with automatic misery I raised my eyes to my Kaaba pleading for it to pity a lovestruck young man. A feeling that a miracle must be about to happen now clawed at me; **a gentle hand landed on my shoulder: "Can you please let me hang this clipping," the girl asked me shyly.**

A Gentle Touch from a Girl

Her gentle touch startled me aside as one who had been shocked by electricity. My forehead beaded as I made room for her. I did not utter a single word. I imagined the poor girl could feel my heartbeats pulsing and the roar of my blood boiling. We were alone when I pierced her with shining eyes like arrows that flustered her and caused her to redden from astonishment.

She understood after a moment that I was interested in the clipping in her hand and not what showed of her slender figure, so she set about fixing her clipping to the board and proceeded to withdraw.

A Sly Deed

I took advantage of our solitude, as I must commit a deed that was not in my habit. I kept watching as the girl's movement at long last disappeared from sight, so I could commence my deed safely. I stood alone in front of a miracle coming true; I decided to commit the deed and hide the clipping from everyone – this job was for me, and me only.

I stripped it off lightly and meanly.

I stripped off the clipping and rushed to the public phone to call the number; it was my habit to send my CV by fax then call afterwards, and they would tell me that the job was no longer vacant. This time I would call first and be the first; let's see who would beat me, and who would? A cunning smile ascended my lips as I stuffed the clipping into my pocket!

A Conversation I Had Long Waited For

"Hello, sir, I just heard that you are looking for a trainee in your office. I have excellent grades, and I was hired as a Teaching Assistant at the Hebrew University."

"Very nice. Are you sure of these statements? Send us your CV immediately and let's set an interview quickly; we are in dire need of you. Send it by fax and call me directly. I'm waiting for you."

Fate has finally smiled upon you, boy!

Come, oh happy day, come… my heart jumped in joy; fate has finally smiled upon you, boy!

The only democracy in the Middle East

My Jewish colleagues would beat me to apply. That was the reason for the refusals, nothing else. For a moment

I almost believed what Arabs would circulate about racism in the state of Israel, the only democracy in the Middle East; it was just a matter of first-come first-served. **Ah, how naive and pessimistic I was!**

Face-to-Face with the Logic of Racism

"Hello, sir, this is Rami again. Has my CV reached you? I called you a minute ago, how are you? When shall I come by to meet you?"

"The job? It's no longer available," he replied with noticeable coldness.

"Sir, we spoke only one minute ago, and you were very eager, and you've just published your advertisement. What happened now? Was it my name that changed your mind?"

"You're not what we're looking for," … He hung up the phone with a sharp tone.

No doubt he had realized now why no one had scooped me up until now, because those who excel are snatched away as if abducted. That was the secret behind his initial eagerness and the secret behind his secondary disappointment.

The blows of racism are painful.

That was the first racist blow I had received in my life. My body shook with fury and my eyes flooded with helplessness; neither my grades nor my excellence saved me.

Surprises might not all be happy or bad.

At home I was used to looking for my old coat and finding my lost hat. I imagined life to be a similar case; you look for something like a job vacancy and find a surprise instead, but I never pictured that **the surprise would be a landmine of racism that would explode in my face this way.**

The hero does not die at the beginning of the film.

As a distinguished student, I resorted to private lessons, tutoring university students older than me, teaching them the abstruse incantations of economics and accounting, and I miserably watched my Jewish students as the offers were heaped on them without me.

My father hid a hurtful truth from me.

The headline was clear on the vacancies board, but I ignored it. I noticed every slight change and eyed every new advertisement, but I did not notice a very important matter: that I was Arab. My father did not tell me what that meant when I was little. Perhaps he did not want to hurt my feelings. Many things I learned by myself through the longest way and the worst method.

Because I don't want you to suffer as I have suffered.

My friend,

You are not suffering alone. I have also suffered, and my path was not paved with roses as you might think, and it is one of the reasons that pushed me to finish writing this book, so that the largest number of people can benefit from my life lessons and morals – people who have gone through or are going through moments of weakness, poverty, misery, desperation, or racism. When I relay my experiences truthfully, I help you to correctly read your life book and to see the world clearly.

We can change the world.

Be confident, we can change our lives and the world around us when we understand matters from all their social, economic, and humanitarian aspects in a practical fashion that grants us the tools that let us free ourselves from the gravity of the vicious circle in whose orbit we revolve and revolve.

The hero does not give up!

I did not give up at that point, and I decided to go back to searching for a job vacancy. I had to finish two years of training to be able to practice my profession; I had to hold tightly to my dream and not let circumstances rule me.

Despite the political, military, and religious complications... nothing is impossible.

To find a job vacancy for an Arab in the Hebrew Jerusalem, the capital and address of religious zealotry, and the stage for struggles and bombings, was not an easy matter at the time; I have told you about Bus 26 that exploded and from which I escaped by a miracle.

At last, and after laborious effort… in a city worn down by historical conflicts.

In that year, 1999, and after laborious effort, I found an internship at a public account auditors' office in the west side of the city, as Jerusalem has an eastern Arab side and another western Hebrew side. Racism made me resort to accept joining the first office that accepted my Arabness.

I contacted an office owned by two Jewish partners at the beginning of their lives, and by chance one of them was named Rami. They agreed to invite me for a job interview, and that was my first job interview since I started sending out my CV to the offices across the city over weeks of ceaseless attempts, in a city worn down by Arab-Hebrew struggle and in which racism nests and grudges hatch.

After hardship there is only succor.

I snapped up the invitation immediately, and my happiness was too great for words. That invitation had come at a time of great need and on a deep, yet unhealed wound. I got ready for the interview with a formal suit and perfumed myself with everything within my reach.

The locks of agony and the cement of wretchedness

I arrived for the interview exactly at the agreed time. The two partners met me with a smile, and after an amiable meeting and professional questions, they found what they were looking for in my person, as my accomplishments and fluency pleased them, so they agreed to employ me at a difficult personal time, **when despair was getting the best of me.**

Why do I describe my happiness at the job to you?

I gave out sweets and received congratulations from all parts. I mention all this so you can realize how much **this job meant to me, until I imagined it to be my coronary artery**, and it never occurred to me to leave a job that could not be replaced ever.

And the moment of the test arrived.

The first exams for the first semester of the fourth year approached. That was a preparatory test for the government licensing test. All my peers got a whole month's leave from their work offices; the material was rich and thorny and especially for those who worked and studied-- we had to review what was difficult or what we missed of topics because of the pressures of work.

Severe Obstinacy

As for where I worked, they refused to grant me leave for more than two weeks. I pleaded with them without result; they claimed that the material did not need more than that. "You're smart and we've tried this subject and one of us got a medal of excellence in it." My attempts did not convince them, and I felt severe unease because I knew for certain that the material could not be covered within two weeks.

The logic of cowardice wins.

I was not able to object because of the fear of losing the irreplaceable job of a lifetime, as I imagined it.

And the stunning occurrence took place.

What a disaster! For the first time I failed completely in a university subject. My grade was not so very far from the highest grade, but failure in itself was for me a great calamity.

The news of the grades being posted reached me while I was at work; that day I called my roommate Alaa and asked him to rush to the board and bring me the good news. I accompanied him on the phone as he checked my grade. He was struck by an agitation that shook the phone's speaker, and he knew that I was a top student.

A Disastrous Conversation

He asked me, "Are you sure of your ID number?"

I said with hurry, "Yes."

He said falteringly, "Maybe there's a mistake!"

I said, "Don't worry, this is an extremely hard test; what's important is that I pass 60%."

And he responded with a quick finality as one who casts a burning coal from his hand, "Your grade is a Fail."

Oh, The Scandal, Oh My Woe!

The phone dropped from my hand. I asked permission to leave work and dashed to the board like a madman. I checked, inspected, scrutinized, rechecked, rummaged, ransacked…

Indeed, I had failed.

Oh, the disaster and scandal… if it were not for the fact that more than two-thirds of the students had failed the subject, I might have had a heart attack.

I gathered my crumbling strength and took myself back to the student dorms, suppressing the disappointment that appeared on my pale visage. I slept that night the sleep of one bereaved and distressed.

Someone who is wet does not fear the rain.

I had to take my anger out on someone. There was no longer anything I dreaded; I went to work early and went in to the partner who was there and gave him my resignation, but not before I exploded in his face with anguish.

I said: Because of you I failed for the first time in my life. All the students in all the offices in the nation got a month to study except for me. You've destroyed my pride and shaken my confidence.

He replied: Take it easy, there's no need to worry. You're not alone. The failure rate exceeded 70%. There's a retake exam – you'll definitely pass it.

I said: I don't care about the retake now. I care that I failed because of working for you.

He said: Don't rush to resign. We'll give you a full month's leave for the retake.

I said: I don't want to work in a place that was the cause of my failure.

He said: We can't let you go so easily. You've mastered a lot of matters in a brief time, and we've come to depend on you. Take a vacation from now and another month or two months to calm down, and we will compensate you for what happened with loose and flexible work hours, and we will discuss the pay later.

I said: I no longer have any desire to work in your office.

My pride is not a place for negotiation.

I refused all offers and inducements, and left the job of a lifetime, and went on my way in revenge for my broken pride.

I won't forget the lessons of this snapshot from the book of my life. Suddenly…

Fear left me, **and I became the master of myself** and owner of my fate.

The **job was no longer my lifeline**, even though it had come at a time of great need and replacing it seemed near impossible, because there's an alternative to everything.

I **discovered my skills** and the need my job had for my abilities, which I had not noticed before.

I **knew well my self-worth**, and I became able to negotiate and lay conditions, and I broke the one-sided equation!

I **respected myself** and valued it, so I imposed my respect and value on them.

I **freed myself from my slavery** to my job and work, and the job no longer owned me!

I **freed myself from the fear** that had chained my thoughts and made me fall into a delusional captivity.

I learned **leaving my job was no longer a disaster nor the end of the world.**

I became certain **that change only needs courage** to overcome the fear of turning on the light switch.

it was proven to me **that showing your weakness and need will make people shortchange you and take advantage of you.**

Life had taught me lessons through a stunning disaster; it led it to me so I could wake up from my heedlessness and free me from the captivity of the job.

The Worst Nightmare University Film of the Year 1995, Starring Myself

The stations of our life surprise us with wonders that we had not accounted for. That obliges us to arm ourselves with the tools of awareness and knowledge of what we are approaching, and it obliges us to benefit from the experiences of others generally, and from our experiences specifically.

The Skill of Expecting the Worst and the Best

There's no harm in practicing the skill of "expecting the worst and the best." Let your mind soar in the possibilities and expect the worst cases and the best ones. You could find that the risk won't be costly to the degree of breaking your back no matter how much bad luck frowns in your face, or that the benefit is not worthwhile to a sufficient extent no matter how much chances smile upon you, **so why should you undertake a deal whose profit is in the best of cases meager? Or draw back from a deal which will not in its worst cases lose?**

Loss of Confidence is a Destructive Blight

This skill does not only make us step with confidence, but it also saves us from falling into an astonishment that shakes our balance when we achieve an unexpected failure.

The sudden imbalance could make you lose confidence in yourself and your skills and in others; loss of confidence is a destructive blight which hinders chances that heal you from an emotional, professional, domestic, or financial crisis.

University Hooligans… The Mo'adon Gang

How much my childhood heroics helped throughout the period of my university studies, as it made me acclimate to dealing with predators of the hooligan variety. I never in my life pictured that I would meet them roaming around freely and comfortably in the areas of the university campus and inside the student dorms.

Students who were addicted to the "club" (*Mo'adon* in Hebrew), a club for playing snooker and drinking alcohol and "having fun." Supposedly it was a recreational facility for the university students to relieve the stresses of studying, but with time hooligans in the dress of students took control of it and turned it into a hideout.

A Hideout on Campus

It sits in a desolate corner between the buildings of the student dorms. The shadows of dancing red and blue lights spot its windows. It is shaded by clouds of smoke from the trains of hookahs, the spreading scent of their sweetened tobacco melding with perfumes and alcohols that stuff up one's nose and turn one's stomach, and with cackles that splits apart the tranquility of the night to the beat of boisterous music and the clacks of snooker cues.

Oh, the wretchedness of whoever has for a roommate one of the scoundrels from the "Mo'adon" gang!

A Grind, or "*Harshan*" in Hebrew

Don't believe that the university student differs too much from the children you knew in your youth; you will discover this from the first day. Prepare yourself for the worst. You will find in it the bitter and the sweet, and the lazy and the diligent.

Do you remember how the hooligan boys used to call me by the nickname "neurotic" in my youth because I was very studious?

University Students Are Like Children and Worse

You will find university students who are not less than children in hooliganism; they call you a grind or "*harshan*" in Hebrew as if it were an insult, with the goal of detracting from your person and injuring your determination and diligence, out of envy from themselves; they don't want you to excel and study while they are playing.

The Reznik Dorms for University Students

Acceptance into the Meirsdorf building, known as the Reznik student dorms, was the dream of first year students. Steps separate you from campus; there's no need to follow the bus schedules, no need to get up early, and you don't worry about returning before transportation services stop, because one jump and you're in the university, and one jump from there to your dorm. You will be able to steal a nap or shower or bite, and you might want to escape from a boring lecture.

A Dream Rarely Realized

The dream came true, and I was accepted into the Reznik dorm, building number 9, close to the university by a measure of half a jump only, and without a roommate to bother me or limit me in his sleeping and waking and studying. In short, I received the gift of a lifetime, "a private nearby residence", and I spent the nights and days in comfort, no one annoying me.

Each of us envies the other.

The students envied me for this blessing, and even so, I used to dream of a mate to share the twin room with me, who would entertain me and cheer my homesickness in a university where I did not have many acquaintances. I used to envy them their nights up with their roommates, chatting together and joking, and I would stay up with my radio and papers!

The most beautiful dream turns into the worst nightmare.

One nice day at noon, I jumped to my private room to find bags and clothes lying on the opposite bed, and around the room wafted unmistakable smells that reminded me of the *mo'adon*. I stayed briefly and left for my university.

The Curiosity

I returned after eight in the evening heading to our room, curiosity to know the identity of the new resident possessing me. I knocked at the room against my habit, opened the door stealthily for fear that he might be sleeping or perusing his books, and did not find anyone. It was clear that he had overrun the place and perfumed it with his cigarette. I relaxed on my bed after a warm shower and light dinner like all my dinners.

Abu Shreek

Then I found myself starting to awake at the sound of thumping footsteps and *Mo'adon*-ian cackles, and in came Abu Shreek[7], as he used to call me, and with him the *Mo'adon* gang bursting in on me in our room. I met them up close for the first time and their chief accompanied them; they stirred up a clamor and rent apart the tranquility of the room with their ruckus. The room did not fit the remaining members of the jostling herd, so some of them stood outside the room fouling the dorm lobby, waiting for Mr. Bigshot to perfume himself and get ready for the night out.

I nearly had a stroke.

I nearly had a stroke when I learned that the *Mo'adon* chief, in his *Mo'adon*-ian majesty, would be from today onward "Abu Shreek," my homie.

I turned into the icon of patience.

I became an object of pity and the hero of a joke for the fellows who had wished for my place yesterday. I

---

7   A nickname for one's roommate or partner in a business, akin to calling them "my roomie" or "my homie", or perhaps "pard" as in short for partner.

became an icon of inspiration and patience to students who discovered suddenly that their roommate was not as bad as they had pictured him, and that there is always what is worse. Many now found in me solace!

The most depressing days of my life ever.

A depression that clouded my thinking and hampered my studying took over my life!

I could no longer stand the dorm, and I started to spend the nights in the university library until late at night, and I imposed myself on friends, staying up with them to the point of annoyance, then returning unwillingly to my depressing cell.

Peak Tension

The tension in my relationship with Abu Shreek reached its peak. I was a freshman student and in the highest pinnacles of diligence, and he was a second-year student and the head of the *Mo'adon* of vagrancy.

I could no longer go to sleep.

I had to summon and recall my childhood skills and sense of security. I did not go to sleep until after he fell deeply asleep, then I woke up early to study with puffy eyes surrounded by the black of exhaustion, and he would sleep from dawn till night, and wake up like bats, hurrying to his den.

Sleeping with one eye open.

On a cold night, the exhaustion of suspicion won over me, so I went to bed before the time of his return. I set my alarm for six in the morning, before sunrise, slept the sleep of a wolf with one eye open, and lay under my blanket looking out for his heavy steps as he opened the door dragging the tails of loss. This time a constituent of the gang accompanied him; his identity became apparent from their suspicious whispers.

The Attempt to Get Rid of Me… Save me, my grandfather's den.

They entered quietly and came close to my bed. I glimpsed their feet from under my blanket; they stood over my head exactly, one of them whispering to his drunken companion, "What do you say we finish him off now?" I didn't know if he was holding anything. My heartbeats sped up until they nearly gave me away. Then I remembered my grandfather's den, and I prepared for a surprise reaction in case they attempted some stupidity.

Abu Shreek was not that scary villain in his wakefulness, but they were drunk now and who knew what they might do when they had lost their reason.

The confrontation was imminent and dangerous this time.

"Forget about him now. Let's think of something else," the other whispered as they discussed a way to run me off, and they retreated at last. Then they sufficed themselves with turning off the alarm so I would not wake up for my prayer and my university, and they threw themselves down in surrender to fatigue, oblivious to the world, the chief on his bed and his follower on the floor of the room.

I sighed in relief. I waited until they fell into the sleep of folly and stupor. I did not sleep after that, and bolted to my prayer in panic, not believing what had just happened.

An Urgent Complaint to the Hall Director

At seven in the morning, and at the suggestion of a Jewish neighbor who lived across from me, I was at the door of the residence hall director relating to her what had happened. The dorm policies prohibited letting a stranger stay over, or what the students called "a settler," or "*mitnahel*" in Hebrew.

My neighbor confirmed my story to her and gave witness to my suffering. The director sympathized with my plight and advised me to leave the building as if nothing had happened, and she promised me to put an end to my nightmare in her own way.

I bid them goodbye with a saddened face and happy heart

I returned at the midday naptime and found Abu Shreek half-awake from his drunkenness against his habit, and his companion next to him like a wet chick, bewailing their rotten luck; the hall director had initiated a surprise supervisory raid and so caught them in the act of breaking the "forbidden settlement" rule, and sentenced Abu Shreek to immediate eviction for his violation of the strict official policies.

I showed my astonishment and severe sorrow for their rotten bad luck. I was obliged to remove the suspicion from myself. They did not buy the idea of terrible luck and they did not seem to be convinced by my feigned astonishment. Then I bid them goodbye, to never return, with a saddened face and a joyful heart. I sympathized with their plight as they carried out their bags not knowing where to go.

Before I wrote this book of mine and before I discovered the obscure ciphers that lead the world, I used to wonder:

- How could a smart university student from a respectable family reach this disgraceful state?

- How could you find a student alert when he is awake, wise in his time, going into the thorniest political and humanitarian matters with you; then it's not long before he surrenders so easily to alcohol that does away with his reason and prestige?

- How could a student waste his parents' money and trouble on nights out and vagrancy, while his family at home are waiting for him to return with a degree?

An Obscure Duality

I would meet Abu Shreek shortly after his eviction and exchange small talk about his condition and news with him. He seemed to me simple and kind and naive, and not such a Gargamel to the extent that he had appeared to be. At the time the matter nearly drove me crazy from the duality of the personalities that I used to meet… **the human being is that obscure dual-natured one!**

And after reading my personal book, I should have wondered at myself.

I should not have wondered nor been surprised, as over years and since my early childhood, life had been preparing me for these moments and these snapshots!

Life is an exceptional teacher… It was preparing me from the beginning.

Because my first-grade teacher who destroyed my cheeks and shook my brain with his blows was also a university graduate, and he carried the title, but he was a monster in the guise of a preacher, and my elegant second-grade teacher was a university graduate and a gentle female, but she was a criminal in the costume of an educator.

Then, life had in its way brought me together with university hooligans at a very early age, and what's strange is that it chose to pass these lessons on to my cheeks in my first year in school with the males, and

it repeated them for me in my second year with the females, but I did not comprehend the lesson despite its tough applications and sexual variation.

And what about my return to the street of death and my driving a car without a steering wheel?

Wasn't I a fresh college graduate the day I committed that deadly stupidity?

Wasn't that a practical lesson that explained and interpreted many of the incorrect and crazy logics that don't differentiate between young and old or ignorant and learned? You let them ride you and lead you to your demise without you being aware, and the whole way to the guillotine you think that you are doing good work, and that you're exerting a brave and wise endeavor?

What are the logics that could compel students to walk the ways of hooligans?

The logic of "He's a kid, let it go" could be one of them… because a doctor is a doctor whether they graduate with an average of 60% or 100%, and an engineer is an engineer whether they study and work hard or sleep and go wild. The university gown hides underneath it every vice and offense.

And with the spread of the variety of professional insurances and legal interpretations, an error in the diagnosis of a patient or engineering of a building or consultation in investment is no longer a crime that causes the world to heave nor an enormous loss nor a major scandal, so why should they work hard and tire themselves then?

And do you remember the secret of the number 40?

Some students depend on their mother and father like the Israelites depended on the Lord.

And they might think that life is coincidence and luck!

A Nearly Unbelievable Joke

Do you know how university dorms are? As soon as it's known that there is a vacant dorm, especially if it's close to the university, the settler students fall upon it to snap up the chance, after they had gotten fed up with leeching off friend after friend, as whoever receives them takes a risk by committing an infraction punishable by certain eviction; but even so it was a calculated risk, because the management did not purposefully overrun the student dorms or forcibly ambush them searching for the homeless, unless they received a tip-off or someone's luck was severely cruddy.

Excuse me… I've come for you!

I was still holding back my crocodile tears over parting with "Abu Shreek" when that same night an old new vagrant came to visit, one of the members of the gang and a close friend to Abu Shreek, dragging his bags and coming in with the "ahem" of provocation and the "excuse me" of vexation, jubilant and happy with his new residence, and greeted me with his colloquial language, "How are you, Abu Shreek?"

Abu Shreek had told him about his incident and urged him to submit an instant application for residence on the basis of a vacant place…

And just as you departed you've returned.

And the gang's monkeying returned to disturb my sleep and irk my life, and once again I became the object of a joke, bandied about in student environments with a mockery that did not lack sorrow and humor.

I laughed today as I have never laughed before as I remembered the lines of my book.

A tactical retreat is a profit not a flight!

It is not wise to continue a battle or insist on a deal that will cost you more than you will benefit. The gang had set me in their sights after I had betrayed the chief and his close follower. They were not going to leave me until they had chased me out in the dead of night.

I could have been stubborn, but the price will be exorbitant when you battle those who have nothing to lose or fear for. I had my studies, my concentration, my mental state, my sleep… and they had none of that, drinking and boozing as if tomorrow would never come.

An exchange deal… not a fair one but a winning one.

In the end I withdrew from my dorm and moved to a dorm in another building. I exchanged residence with a student whose roommate had worn him down also. I haggled him for his roommate and he haggled me for mine, and after negotiations between the four sides, we signed an exchange deal wherein I moved to the far dorm. My new roommate was not easy for my heart to digest, and the dorm was also further.

The Benefits Function

The comparison was between the loss resulting from the exchange deal and between what I would have lost if I had resisted and stayed. It was an unfair deal on the scale of bare numbers, but it was winning in the calculation of the benefits function… Do you remember the lesson of the economics of benefits?

Life examples are many:

- **One might be reluctant to sell a stagnant merchandise at its cost price or a little less;** he does not want to lose anything, so he does not relent, and he insists on resisting the market until its price falls to rock bottom or it wears out, so he loses his entire capital as a result of stubbornness and pride.

- **Even if you are in the right,** flaming up discussions in charged situations, with your son or wife or employee or president, could lead to estrangement and divorce and an enormous loss. At that point, tactical retreat would be a wisdom that averts a bigger harm, and if you will, remember the wise Prophet's instruction, **"I guarantee a house in the surroundings of Paradise for a man who avoids quarrelling even if he were in the right."**

- **Remember Khalid bin Al-Waleed's leadership and his stubborn logic?** He never lost a battle in his life, but in the Battle of Mu'tah he retreated with military shrewdness, extricating an army of 3,000 warriors from the claws of 200,000 warriors who besieged them, and people called them runaways. The Prophet, the commander-in-chief of the forces, said **"They are not runaways but rather repeaters!"**

- **The Treaty of Hudaybiyyah is maybe the biggest example in human history;** people saw it as submissiveness and cowardice, and Al-Faruq[8] was the most severe of people in opposition to its illogical clauses, and even the great Prophet's clarifications were not successful in putting out Al-Faruq's rage,

---

8   Also known as Umar ibn al-Khattab, al-Faruq is one of Prophet Muhammad's companions, and the second Islamic caliph.

until the high Lord intervened with Quranic verses in which He called the illogical treaty a "conquest," and it was indeed a clear conquest!

The Relationship between University Hooliganisms and World Tragedies

Some of those hooligans today assume positions, holding on to nations' hinges, monopolizing decisions of war and peace. For a brief time, I battled local politics at a downscaled town level, and I have followed the conduct of many major politicians at the world level, and especially those who have ravaged and are ravaging the earth with corruption.

Trace for yourself their life book to know the logic that controls them, and when you uncover their cipher, you will understand how they see their monstrous crimes as the eye of reason and the pinnacle of humanitarianism!

Hold on. I mean their life book, not their written biography.

The difference is vast. The biography they write is a big lie, as it is possible to cover crimes and mistakes of the past, present, and future with a university gown, official suits, neckties, elegant feminine makeup, and a suave logic.

Today there are guidance workshops that prepare you for job interviews. They refine you so that you appear to be different from your reality. We practice

the logic of ciphers to bewitch the people around us with all methods and ways. Companies similarly depend on your life biography, but they also try hard to uncover your cipher through interviewing you and tracing your tracks!

Your True Book

The resume whose details begin at the moment of your graduation and are limited to enumerating your areas of expertise is not your true book. Your true book is the tiniest details of your life in your childhood and adolescence and university and work, and the best expertise is your life experiences that you have experienced and lived with!

Warning... Modern Electronic Devices to Uncover Your True Biography

Today, commercial companies and work bosses and even the owners of sport clubs no longer suffice themselves with your curriculum vitae and technical skills.

Civil and governmental factions and gangs form that specialize in tracking and sniping and analysis. They follow your data and movements and tweets and likes and relationships from your youth, and they care for the finest details of your life that people relate about you, and that you relate yourself to people on your pages through your pulpit presentations and electronic sermons.

And today, the process of collecting data is considered the sole source of income for some companies specializing in this startling skill.

Your Electronic Biography

Your electronic biography will determine your future without you being aware or meaning to. The world is being pushed toward this canyon. It is more truthful and more dangerous than any biography that you compose to send to a party courting their affection, and you must take warning and warn those around you from its danger on our future and the future of our works and projects.

You don't know who is looking at your data now and drawing your picture for the intended circles. Use the weapon of ciphers to your advantage!

Fishing Rods and Intercontinental Targeted Missiles

By the action of technological advancement and digital spying, it has become possible to target any sector – of generation, sex, color, and environment – in the world, not only at the level of commercial marketing, **but even at the level of interfering with nations' politics and their internal affairs.**

The Russian interference that was alleged in the 2016 American elections for example and the spread of the phenomenon of **Human Social Bots** or social media spammers that fill the channels of the web to influence the world consciousness and the prevalent logic are examples of a war of unconventional weapons, in which the ciphers of human logic are used in an obvious or obscene fashion.

The relationship of my withdrawal in front of the gang with the world of politics:

It's not a secret that the people with the most judicious minds and sound opinions usually withdraw from the political arena, just as I withdrew in front of the hooligans of the *Mo'adon*. I had a lot to lose – my studies, reputation, family, and rest – and so is the political plaza as well; whoever enters it could lose their studies, reputation, family, and rest!

Therefore, many withdraw like I withdrew, and this way matters remain in the hands of the hooligans, and this might explain many of the international behaviors and world politics that don't differ from the behaviors of the beasts of the forests!

Oh, if only I had read my life book before entering university!

I learned the lesson only in my second year in university. I chose my roommate beforehand according to what the clauses of the dorm policies permitted. At least I did not let life strike me again like it struck me in the second grade of elementary school!

If I had known that there are hooligans in university, I would have kept the matter of my dorm's vacancy in the fold of secrecy and silence or searched for a roommate myself before the axe fell!

There are no gaps in life and no stillness, because if you don't fill the gap someone else will fill it, and if you don't move on life's board to wherever you choose for yourself, some scoundrel will move you to wherever they choose for you.

And here I was ousted for the same reason.

But I left matters to lead me toward them. I ignored the lesson of turning on the light near my hand. I stood still like a statue in my place of residence waiting for a miracle to bring me a roommate according to my whim to cheer my loneliness, and I forgot the lesson of indifference for which I was fired from my work in the worst way, and here I was being ousted from my dorm for the same stupid reason.

A surprising pivotal lesson: Solitude is not the worst choice.

There is no failure in life. Even failed experiences are lessons and morals that prepare you for a coming phase. Sometimes we cannot realize the truth of matters except by saddening or painful practical experiences. Don't despair and don't be distressed. Be confident that your current reality with its joys and miseries is only a preparatory lesson for events that await you at the next junction or nearby corner!

Choosing My Life Partner

The disastrous withdrawal taught me that solitude was not the worst choice. Your life without a partner might be better by far than a partner that vexes your living, and this was the reason for my deliberation in choosing my life partner; there was no harm in spending some time as a bachelor over rushing to choose a partner who does not suit me.

Know when to withdraw.

The timing of withdrawal is an important factor. It's important to withdraw at the appropriate time and before it's too late. Because of the residence crisis a lot of subjects accumulated on me, and I had to withdraw before the beginning of the exam period. Delaying the decision or tarrying in concluding the deal would have exposed me to definite losses and dangers!

Economic Partnerships: Incorrect Investment Logic

Despite the lessons that we go through, we might yet make a mistake at the time of application, **and we like to attribute the cause to impulsivity or over-eagerness, and this is not at all accurate, because the real cause is rather an incorrect cipher we have gotten used to.**

When we get used to an incorrect logic then it can become an indisputable reality within the subconsciousness that directs us.

The logic of my friendships is incorrect.

And this is indeed what happened to me. I rushed to enter an investment partnership with a dear friend. Friendship had a large role in my being struck with blindness, or rather turning a blind eye, because we overlooked conditions and qualifiers that foretold an implicit failure for that partnership. Friendship is one thing and economical partnerships are an entirely different thing.

When a friend accompanies you from the first moments of your childhood, when you've spent together the most beautiful moments and the most miserable, and he always stood by your side and you stood by his, you would argue but how quickly you would make up. **Then that could develop in you both an incorrect logic that has no connection with the commercial reality, so you mistakenly conclude that a successful friendship must necessarily result in an ideal economic partnership, but how quickly the explosion occurs.**

Even if you're the best friends in the world.

When you have a financial and investment strategy that differs from your partner's vision, the partnership cannot continue, even if you were the best friend in the world, and if it continues it will be unwillingly, like the partnership of two contentious spouses, neither the children nor the neighbors sleeping except to the din of their constant shouting.

The Embarrassing Separation

In the end, there was no escaping the dissolution of the partnership with my lifetime friend, despite the severe embarrassment that accompanied the separation. That is neither a disgrace nor a detraction. We had differing visions in the field of business. It is impossible for a ship to be conducted by two captains who have two different destinations. **We had to announce the separation before that partnership destroyed our brotherly relationship and obliterated a long lifetime friendship.** That was another lesson in the quiver of my experiences.

Incorrect Importation Logic: I Lost Millions of Dollars in One Deal

And once more the incorrect logic led me to an uncalculated rush.

I signed several trade deals in the field of importation, at a time when importation was not prevalent and the sites for buying and selling were not well-known or widespread, and there were no guarantees like the ones exchange sites offer today, and so I took a lot of risks and ventured into deals with personalities from the east of the world to the west.

A Direct Punch Which Stuck Me to the Corner of the Ring

This spawned in me a blind confidence in an incorrect investment logic which led me unawares to a trade deal that did not cost me much, but it aimed a direct punch at me that stuck me to the corner of the ring and uncovered a network of imposters to me.

I contracted with a company for the importation of an in-demand commodity from India. They had an innovative website and competitive prices. I communicated with the Indian embassy in the country, and they told me that the company is well-known and seems to them to be serious, and I became eager for this assumption without thinking too much.

Preparations and Arrangements

I received a sample by air mail that confirmed the needed quality, and I began to arrange the distribution network in the country. Everything was ready to snap up the merchandise, and luck appeared to be gaping its mouth after my communication with a huge importation and distribution company. I became eager for the price in an unexpected fashion.

Apprehensions Bridled by Incorrect Logic

I had some apprehension, so I requested the company that we start with a quarter of the decided quantity and at the same unit price as the whole quantity as a proof of its seriousness, so they set a condition in return that the payment be by direct bank transfer to an American bank, instead of paying by a conditional bank order, or Letter of Credit (LC).

A simplified professional definition:

A Letter of Credit, or conditional bank order, is a conditional payment, on the basis of which the buyer deposits the amount in an accredited bank which acts as an intermediary in the deal, and in return for the deposit the bank releases a letter to the seller, on the basis of which the bank pledges to release the amount to the seller's account at the moment that the conditions set out in the letter are fulfilled. Usually, the condition is set to be the arrival of the merchandise to the port of entry, or any condition set by the importer to guarantee the arrival of their merchandise safe and whole.

And this way the buyer guarantees the arrival of the merchandise to their hand, and the seller guarantees the arrival of the money to their pocket.

I transferred $8,000.

I transferred an amount of $8000 indeed. I received the shipping documents, and everything seemed to be as they should.

If this deal succeeded, then it would be the prelude to deals in the hundreds of thousands of dollars, and I along with my partners would be only intermediaries, counting the millions as we sit cross-legged in our offices.

The shipment was delayed past its decided time, and I kept in constant communication with the company, who assured me that everything was as they should be.

A Sudden Punch Below the Belt

My suspicion grew. I communicated with the shipping company and sent them the shipping document. I received an urgent call from a company employee telling me that the document was forged, and the embassy denied its responsibility toward the company. I found out from the shipping company that I had not been the first victim but for my good luck I was the one with the least loss. They told me about victims from Lebanon and neighboring countries who had lost tens of thousands of dollars at the hand of the same fictitious company.

Incorrect logic is ingenious at putting down rebellions.

All the red lights were blinking in warning, but the incorrect logic that I gained through the profits realized by blind deals before it made me confident in the success of this deal as well, ignoring all the warnings and lessons that I took through my study of economics and accounting and world trade, especially since the invested amount had not been of a size that called for much worry.

And I lost the millions!

I did not only lose $8,000 that day, but I lost millions of dollars that I actually touched and counted in my dreams.

My mother taught me, and the mother of the world taught me.

My mother taught me, and the Mother of the World (as Egyptians describe their country) taught me, unforgettable cipher lessons:

The First Theft I Committed… A Cipher Lesson from My Mother

On my way home from school, it was a habit of mine to push open the gate and sneak into the courtyard of my maternal uncle's house. I would spy on the chickens in the coop, watching them from outside its window that overlooked the courtyard and following their movements.

One day, I found a chicken close to the coop window. I watched it until it laid an egg near my hand; I hesitated before I reached out my hand, then I made up my mind and grabbed the egg, and I withdrew, hiding the spoil in my bag.

But how would I resolve the matter with my mother?

I went around our house and gathered some straw around the egg, and then went in to my mother calling: "Mom, come see what I found behind the house."

She followed me, knowing it was a chicken egg, but hid the fact that she knew from me and began to coax me into talking, until I spilled the beans, and the shocking judgment came: **You must return it to its place!**

And how could I return it? I might be discovered; I had to push open the door and carry the egg to the end of the long courtyard – what would I tell them if they caught me?

I begged her to let me off and return it herself, but she insisted that I return it by myself; she had uncovered my cipher, as she was my mother.

And my mother told me a story of folklore about a thief who cut off his mother's tongue – how matters start from an egg and you never know where they end.

A Thief Who Cut Off His Mother's Tongue (A Folklore Story)

Before his death sentence for crimes of murder and robbery was carried out, the last wish he asked for was to see his mother, **so his mother came and ascended the execution scaffold while he was bound. He asked her to put out her tongue for him, and he bit it until he cut it off.**

Those present went crazy over his lack of dutifulness and terrible deed as he was saying goodbye to the world on the execution scaffold.

So, he cried: When I returned to the house with the first egg I stole, my mother ululated in happiness, and from that day I became skilled in theft until I became a criminal and a serial killer. **I have cut off the tongue that ululated the first time and brought me to the hangman's rope.**

She did not leave me any chance, as she was my mother, and she knew how to coerce me.

I was very shy, and I preferred to be hit over being caught in the act of a disgraceful deed, but oh well, my mother insisted.

The Strikes of Shame and Regret!

I returned to the courtyard of my uncle's house with one leg taking me forward and the other backward, pouring sweat in the summer of a hot day, the redness of shame rising in me and the shivers of dread taking over me. I snuck in with the egg shaking in my hand. I hurried toward the coop window with a pounding heart, and I returned the egg without anyone noticing me. I sighed in relief, and took myself back to the house, shame and regret striking me over what happened.

She did not strike me physically, but my mother struck me with the cipher of shame, and so that was the first and last theft in my life.

Lying – A Cipher Lesson from the Egyptian Captain

In 1988, I joined a bootcamp for teaching computer science in Egypt. It extended for three weeks during the summer vacation in August, near the beginning of 7th grade.

In one of the theoretical classes, the captain, as we used to call him, explained to us the graph of the function (x, y), and I did not understand the topic, so I asked him again but I still did not understand.

On the third time and to get rid of him, I said "yes" in response to his question of whether I had understood the explanation, and I did not expect that he would ask me to make sure that I had really understood.

In a hot seat!

But woe betide me, he asked me, and I answered him incorrectly, so he said, "So you did not understand. You've lied, Rami."

He did not care that I had not understood. He only cared that I had lied.

He took to berating me in front of everyone: Why did you lie, Rami? And how could you allow yourself to lie, Rami? And who taught you to lie, Rami? And is this the first time you've lied, Rami? And how can I believe from today going forward, Rami? And how can I trust you, Rami?

Woe betide Rami!

He made me feel that I had committed a great catastrophe and an unforgivable crime, even though I had not meant to lie. I only felt embarrassed in front of him and the students because of his repeated explanation for my sake without me understanding.

If Only My Mother Had Never Given Birth to Me

Then he dismissed everyone and kept me behind. He gave me a long, expansive lecture that exhausted me from shame of my deed. If only I had never lied, and if only my mother had never given birth to me!

That was a cipher lesson in the crime of lying that I learned from Egypt, the Mother of the World, as I learned a lesson in the crime of theft from my tender mother!

The publication of my book was delayed a quarter of a century since 1993!

Since 1993, in twelfth grade, when my teacher, whom I told you about, signed my essay topic – in which I described a fresh event that happened to me in the last summer break – and he wrote for me in his handwriting "**A topic worthy to be published**" – that was not a passing sentence like today, and it did not mean publishing with the click of a button like today!

There were three main journals through which publications were made only. There was no internet in the world nor Facebook or Twitter or smartphones, and no free platforms that all and sundry could ascend. And when the advice came from a poet and writer and professor of the Arabic language, that meant a lot.

That advice was a free lesson that took more than a quarter of a century for me to apply, and I have not included in my book that fresh occurrence that won the admiration of my teacher.

The book produced itself by itself!

And today, the production of this book of mine in the middle of my fourth decade, and after waiting all this time period, is evidence of the success of the book's idea.

The idea of the book is what led me to write it finally even if 26 years later, and if it were not for the book's idea I would not have been able to take control of the delusional obstacles and the incorrect logic that was preventing me from even thinking of writing.

The book's idea made me get rid of complexes that prevented me, and logics that paralyzed me from moving and thinking in the correct direction that would serve my goals. I can say that the book produced itself by itself.

Welcome to my fishing rod!

The fact that you have read this far in the book is another evidence of the success of its idea. Like a fish it caught and lured you, using your very own human cipher!

And now this benefit is sufficient for you:

Here I've given you a magic rod, rather an extraordinary fishing net, and guided you on how to catch the impossible with it and imprison it within your hands. No barrier or impediment will stand in your way after today; you are from today onward the master of yourself, your fate in your hands. You've just been freed from the grip of the false idol that held you prisoner with the sorcery of its cowardly spells and frightened you with the ramming horns of delusion.

Your next step:

To make yourself available to read the next book, written by and starring you. Read it in its smallest details; correct the wrong logics that you have left to lead your steps to where you did not intend; take the

reins of the logic of leadership and direct it to wherever you want; free yourself from your imprisoning logic!

Destroy the horns of your worshipped god, pull him down from the throne of his kingdom, and roar at the top of your voice announcing: I am the knight, and I am the king!

"Completed, with God's help, favor, grace, excellence, and generosity"

Rami Anabusi

RENOUNCING HOLY LOGIC

Treasures and Pearls

Selected from

the Four Acts

"TREASURES AND PEARLS SELECTED FROM ACT I"

- The events in your life are practical lessons, instructional courses at the highest levels, tailored exactly for you with precision and skill.

- There is no single answer in life.

- **You cannot simply jump to final conclusions just because a certain idea occurred to you or a certain logic appealed to you, or just because you caught your child, your spouse, or your colleague red-handed in a disgraceful situation. Similarly, you cannot sign a trade deal simply because you drool over it nor refuse it because of a gut feeling.**

- There aren't only four directions.

- Listen to your son as a father, pay attention to your daughter as a mother, consult your life partner, do not ignore your students as a teacher, do not ridicule your employee as a manager, search between the lines and behind the fence. Do not stop digging and drilling even if everyone tells you, "It's impossible, there's no benefit to be had, and someone smarter would have done it before."

- **A small child taught me a lesson – do not be hasty, do not be contemptuous, do not be**

dismissive, do not to be haughty. She taught me to listen well, consider all the choices, and not insist as though I had all the answers.

- You are the bravest, the most beautiful, and the most loyal. All you need is to have the courage to embark on an exciting adventure to discover yourself, to search for the innocent child lost inside of you, and to rescue the young genius whom the blows of life buried, whom the rebukes of teachers, parents, colleagues, and admonishers silenced. They wanted you lesser and lost.

- Get up and start over again. Don't be afraid of new beginnings, because they will certainly lead you to other new beginnings and paths.

- When you draw for your child a single goal in life, you give them a single way of life, one path without an alternate route. Through the lens of academic excellence, don't be surprised when they don't take other matters with the seriousness you had wished for.

- **Don't regret a train you missed**, milk spilled, time past, or business opportunity forfeited; you don't know what future you were shielded from. Grief will not help you.

- Embrace the new beginning, ride the next wave, move forward without looking back.

- Ignore the suspicious looks, hold your temper. Being different means that you are unique. Don't let discrimination stop you. Your life's book has only one author – you. It only has one pen, the one in your hand. Your decisions and behaviors are the ink it is going to be written with. You are the most important reader of your book, and its greatest beneficiary.

- Be assured, you won't die before your time. Even if you were to knock on death's door with all your might or run at it full-speed.

- Life lessons are like this. They often start with simple lessons, a gentle and safe method of teaching, but if we do not benefit from these lessons and comprehend them well, then life will teach us the same lessons using a different method, which may be harsher and tougher.

- When you uncover a person's code you will control him.

- If a logic works again and again, that doesn't necessarily mean it's right.

- Reliance on incorrect logic makes breaking away from it difficult.

- There's a way out of every predicament in life.

- The timing factor is important.

- We commit a crime toward our children when we punish them unjustly, relying on fear and intimidation alone. We push them toward incorrect behaviors and delinquency, antithetical to our intentions. We stuff them full of psychological traumas and resentments that eat at their hearts.

- The wrong punishment exacerbates wrong behavior.

- We come across road signs in our path, so what meanings does the warning sign of punishment hold? A leader understands: Go cautiously. A coward understands: Don't try!

- A wrong is not righted by another wrong, compounded with recklessness.

- When you reveal your cards or codes to someone you become susceptible to extortion.

- The precision of life lessons cannot be matched by any film lesson or human development program.

- The importance of rehabilitative punishments, criminal And educational: We might make light of our practical life lessons. The hero of certain real-life events might be a young child, but the outcomes of that occurrence and its practical applications are applicable to all the facets of educational systems, including the penitentiary system.

- Our experiences refine us. Failure should not stop you. It's okay to fall, because you only ever fall onto a moral that saves you from destruction. It is the nature of failure to make you feel upset, because failure uses your fall to cast onto your chest the rock of despair. All you have to do is twitch for the rock to get off you. Get out of the hole you fell into and take from it the moral you fell onto; don't you dare pick up the heavy rock of despair with it, and go on lightly, accompanied by the moral that saved you and will save you from future seasonal falls.

- What is important is to be ready for the next opportunity before it comes to you, for it is better to be ready for an opportunity that doesn't come than for an opportunity to come when you are not ready.

- And know from this moment that in this world, you are the king. Your fate is in your hands.

"TREASURES AND PEARLS SELECTED FROM ACT II"

- Your logical codes being deciphered in a certain area will have only one meaning: your loss has certainly become imminent like an easy meal, because your playing strategy on the stage of life has been uncovered and your movements are expected.

- The cobra is captive not to a charmer who exploits it but rather to a logic that chains it, and it will never be free from the grasp of its charmer as long as it is not liberated from the captivity of the logic that controls its fate.

- They produce a herd whose family members all toil and work for the sake of catching up to the speedy fashion train; it spends all its money and reserves and borrows endless recurring loans for the sake of upgrading a car that's still new, changing a smartphone that's still shiny, and building a grand and towering house.

- The "cancer of craziness" is a cipher manufactured by the giants' machine, which spreads the logic of madness and insanity amongst people.

- Courage is not doing things you've gotten used to doing and which no longer scare you, even if that is fighting a lion!

- When we look at ourselves and the people around us with an elastic, positive logic, we will discover that we have not noticed skills and valor that a rigid, negative logic had buried.

- The wrong logic will lead you forcibly to an unreasonable path full of economic, societal, political, and domestic bumps which perhaps only a chance of fate will save you from!

- When your logic is complexly encrypted and unexpected and your enemy's logic is uncovered to you, the war becomes one-sided, and victory is surely yours no matter how much stronger your enemy is!

- Our successes and failures often reach those around us and affect our families, and this is what compounds our duty and drives us to understand logic and uncover its secrets, attracting prosperity and benefits and shielding from evils and abuses, for our sakes and for the sakes of those in our orbits.

- It's true that uncovering the secrets and codes gives you the tool that allows you to take control of the reins of your life, and even to control the reins of others and of the world, but that will never happen as long as you don't have the desire and the courage to do that.

- Being intelligent does not make you a successful leader.

- The greatest successful people and giants of the market eagerly and fervently snatch up his consultative services, but he does not apply them to his reality and does not take advantage of them to his benefit. He remains merely a shadow or unknown soldier, not because he is ignorant and does not know, but because he is captive to a logic that he knows is incorrect; however, he does not have the daring and desire.

- Life is simple and beautiful with no complications in it. But the wrong human logic practices intimidation and scare tactics on us so that life seems outwardly harsh and complicated; our weak point is the fear of the unknown and our incorrect logic exploits the fear complex in us in order to safeguard its position and keep us captive until we die!

- The Logic of Marvels and the Complex of The Guided One: Many are sitting waiting for a divine miracle to accomplish difficult missions for them. The doctrine or complex of the awaited Guided

One has enticed them; they walk the same path and take the same lanes and ride the same trains then hope to open their eyes onto a brighter morning and happier news and a better life and a more beautiful reality.

- "Renounce" the divinity of logic, and come with me step by step, before the white strand of hair appears.

- We may blame the Israelites and not blame ourselves for miracles or wonders that block our path and whip us so that we can change our behavior. They are free lessons that God drives to us by chance!

- No, we are not forced. Rather, go back to the details of your life; you will find that they were practical lessons and behavioral morals freely driven to you as they were driven to me, but you chose, as I chose, to ignore them and interpret them according to the sleepers' mood. And we let that incorrect logic control our ways and paths, grazing in the valley of the slackers, turning in the orbit of danger, and licking the wounds of poverty and need and failure.

- You need a correct behavioral doctrine so that you can learn, not play around!

- When the reasonable scientific mind collides with an observable self-logic, for the most part and unconsciously, we let the perceptible logic lead our steps, even if it were an incorrect logic contradictory to science and the reasonable. That's because humans by nature lean toward the familiar, even if it's a logic surrounded by dangers or a cause of their hardships and miseries. They fear the unknown which they are unfamiliar with, even if it's proven science and validated scientific reality.

- The smart person and the scientist face life experiences and facts by the tons, which they offer as sacrifices on an altar of worshipped behavioral logic; then all these facts kneel prostrating in service to that despotic logic and nourish its ramming horns.

- The Fission Equation: The pollination of science with leadership logic gives birth to a universal fission equation, the extent of whose effects on your life and society and the whole world are unpredictable.

- Renounce the divinity of the behavioral logic that governs you. Pull it down by force from your throne and place it on the dissection table; break its horns, set its limits and define its role for it, and keep your eyes on its horns so they don't grow again. Only then will you taste the flavor of freedom, and life will smile on you. You will take command of the channels of your present and future in order to control your domestic, daily, and social life as if you had been reborn.

- When the wrong logic leads us, we fail to see validated truths and available chances and profitable deals and keep running after a mirage!

- Life is much simpler than we imagine, and the realization of success is much easier than we picture; there is no need for wonders and over-philosophizing and oversaturated programs.

- We don't move on our own; logic is what moves everyone.

- A Different Logic = A Different Way = A Different Result.

- Realizing the secret and solving the codes grant you magical tools and an extraordinary weapon, but these tools will never benefit you as long as you don't possess the desire to use a unique destructive weapon and the courage to ride the express train from your familiar world to a strange world.

- You need a sound, behavioral doctrine to breach the impossible!

- He is that same mouse man who got used to the logic of mice, so it led him voluntarily to the hole of poverty and need. It is you and me when we possess skills and abilities and accept the logic of lowliness.

"TREASURES AND PEARLS SELECTED FROM ACT III"

- The majority dream of being the cobra man, yet they practice the logic of the mouse man, satisfied by life in the holes.

- How plentiful are failed campaigns, announced and engaged in by many; then the strikes of cowardice and failure don't take long to cripple them time after time. Until a person is struck with despair and stops trying and surrenders, despite his possession of all the tools, experiences, and skills that qualify him for victory and triumph!

- Logic is a human invention; it is a tyrannical overlord and a devastating captor, like a vortex that drags in the drowning or a magical staff for sleepers or a spell that chains idiots. It is not a universal law that cannot be trespassed on or argued with, but we fear its power and dread questioning it, and we avoid trespassing on it or challenging it.

- There is nothing in the world that is illogical; there is an incorrect and crooked logic.

- And there is no logical or illogical law; it's either a law or a logic!

- Because logic is outside the bounds of established

laws, because it's a hypothesis yet to be proven, and it could be absurd or random. When logic becomes proven, it is no longer a logic and has become a scientific fact or universal law.

- Until you absolutely prove the validity of a logic, it remains a hypothesis to be researched and discussed; we should not blindly submit to it without thinking. As long as a logic is not absolutely proven and does not have definitive evidence, it will never be a law except in your imaginative delusions only.

- Those in our orbit consider us kings; they imitate us without thinking and inherit from us the behaviors of success and failure and the logics of wealth and poverty. The coward gives birth to failing and poor people, and the brave gives birth to successful and rich people, just as the ostrich gives birth to ostriches.

- Such is a repressive society; the people around you repress you and don't allow you to think or try. They memorize excuses and barriers that make change impossible; they parrot them, they reiterate them, they repeat them like a broken record. They pass them down by heredity generation after generation as if they were verses from a holy book, and they blast them in your face in one shot; they don't encourage you to venture outside the bounds of the box.

- This is the logic of Auster and Auster's people; like most people, they have knowledge and diverge from it. They see the fatal result and don't repent. The writing is on the wall, but they don't see it. They have a strange indifference; they walk as agreed on one cipher, and a suicidal automatic unexplainable logical line, as if they had been created for hardship, or are being forced, their life decisions out of their hands, and their present and future out of their control.

- We constantly excuse our disappointment with external circumstantial excuses. We give them the status of a sacred god. We convince ourselves with them and chain our will with them, and we use them to defend our poverty, failure, and cowardice; excuses that discourage us from trying and make change seem impossible. That is a false, wrongful god that shows you your cowardice as wisdom and your fear as caution and your poverty as contentment!

- Humans' behavior oftentimes contradicts reason, and reality proves that it's within our ability to forge logic and drive it to make the impossible possible, but for the most part we surrender to the power of logic, leaving it to forge us and drive us toward making the possible impossible!

- Rather, logic is a custom we have become used to by seeing it repeated often, until it became a logic conceded to like an unbreakable fanciful law. These fanciful laws that roost and breed in our heads are what rule us and direct us, but life does not recognize them and does not submit to them.

- For the most part, logic is nothing but a kind of comfortable delusion that we convinced ourselves of; we gave it the standing of scientific fact and proven law so that we can summon psychological reassurance and feel control.

- Logic is a conclusion springing from what we see and are familiar with; it is not governed by a proven and specific law. And because humans don't like to live in dark environments that make them feel a loss of control and disturb their heartbeat, so they continuously and with great effort seek desperately to discover the laws around them. Then when they fail to deduce a clear law, they resort to inventing a psychological imaginary law by which to ease their minds and return to them the delusion of control.

- Logic is not a law but rather outside the law; it could be a fable or a crazy spell.

- You are a creature with free will in the midst of this organized world. No law to chain you can be applied to your existence nor any fact to steer and capture you; it is for you to pick what logics and hypotheses as the tool of your mighty mind leads you to.

- Be Heretical to be Free! You must free yourself from the captivity of the familiar and the inherited that chains your giant mind which no artificial computer can match. This will not happen except through heresy, which does not accept crooked logic and does not believe in irrational myths nor in spells that make you hallucinate in broad daylight.

- The poor draw their logic from the conventions of poverty that stem from an ungrateful, complaining, cowardly, surrendering environment; and the rich draw their logic from the conventions of wealth that stem from an optimistic, adventurous, courageous, defiant environment. Therefore, the poor lives by the logic of the poor and gains poverty and misery, and the rich lives by the logic of the rich and gains wealth and comfort.

- The one who bemoans his luck because they were born poor to stay poor, while there is one who was born with a golden spoon to keep the golden spoon in his mouth. They stone fate with what is not in it and hang the causes of their misfortunes on external circumstances, running away from the responsibility that requires them to take new paths they are not familiar with and obligates them to rebel against a jailer who fetters them with the delusions of an erroneous logic.

- When science proves in some of its excavations that some creatures perhaps evolved their bodies, even if by mutation, and in an essential or nonessential manner, then it's worthier for behaviors and instincts to evolve!

- I won't tell you that there are creatures that have evolved their biological bodies over the ages so they can adapt and survive as they say, but I tell you look at circus animals.

- What's more striking is that you find humans amongst us who are incapable of changing their ways, despite the giant minds they carry over their heads!

- Your skin color, fingerprint, and height of stature are not what define who you are, and you shouldn't let them limit and define you; your reactions and steps are what lead you to where you are now and where you will be after now. The same steps will lead to the same results… so renounce every logic that chains you.

- **In our traditional schools, we've gotten used to every question having only a single correct answer, and that's the answer the teacher wants to hear**, even though life often does not have a single solution. If it did, we would have continued to light fire with stones.

- "The Logic of I": **it is a fierce logic that takes control of its owner and drives them rabid; it's akin to a mad dog that rules its owner and seeks to impose its control and dominance over the logic of other people through any means. It does not discuss, listen, understand, change, adjust, or yield; it imposes the solution to problems by force with the logic of muscles and strong-arming.**

- The management of the world, societies, economies, and relationships requires someone who has a flexible leadership logic, who accepts criticism and discussion and improvement. They don't sanctify logic and don't let it control their behaviors and reactions, and they don't give it the standing of indisputable scientific fact.

- Dear repressor… I won't allow your incorrect logic to straddle me, like it has straddled you, with the whip of menaces and threats that were practiced on you in your childhood, and I won't allow your wild logic to kill the young innovator inside me, and I won't permit it to gag the horse of brave leadership logic that I have straddled.

- Life prepares us for coming opportunities on low flame.

- **No matter how much you rise or fall, and even if you were the president of the greatest empire in the world, you're a victim, and your condition is miserable, whether in the apparent or the hidden; perhaps the perpetrator is a harsh father or stepfather, or a severe mother or stepmother, or an abusive husband or wife, or a repressive teacher or lecturer, or school or university bullies, or an exploitative company manager or work colleagues, or a blackmailing worker or employee, or a brand or drug giant, or a despotic state president or government, or a brutal diplomatic equal or national traitor, or a prosperous but ungracious giver or an ungrateful indigent...The perpetrators are many, the victims are in the millions, whether aware or not.**

- The time has come for you to escape from and discard the role of the victim. The time has come for you to escape from and discard the doctrine of cowardice. The time has come for you to escape from and discard the deification of circumstances. The time has come for you to escape from and discard surrendering to reality.

- The time has come for you to escape from and discard the torture of oppression and the pain of repression.

- **The time has come to renounce the divinity of the logic that chains you, and rebel against the whip that rules you. Break the horns of holy things and halos that enslave you; you were born free and dignified so don't let any human being repress you.**

"TREASURES AND PEARLS SELECTED FROM - THE FOURTH ACT"

- Logic is a war machine that destroys the world: Don't take the power of logic lightly; its effects are not just on the areas of your personal life, but also on world peace.

- Even our father Adam's first sin was caused by a Satanic selfish logic.

- The effects of wrong logic could reach beyond their owner to reflexive circles of family, society, nation, and world, which may not be possible to contain at all.

- Don't fall for the neckties: Follow the struggles of the world around you; political discussions and international summits and intercessions and conferences of war and peace, all of them in neckties.

- Life proves that masks and costumes and veneers and positions don't change the nature of scoundrels and hooligans. Life lessons confirm, and the reasonable logic establishes so.

- Don't regard the small events of your life as childhood leisure memories; they are the mirror of your future and a microcosm of your life path. Rather, childhood is the true picture of life without neckties or makeup. Each experience is a brick that polishes your logic and develops your personality; either you lead it to where you want to get to, or you surrender to it wherever it takes you.

- Accepting the role of the victim is giving up.

- Sports and play are the best educational life lessons.

- Self-confidence is your most important weapon.

- Running away triumphant… Know how to run away.

- Surrendering to the reality of life is the easiest of ways.

- Human childhood is a real, bare, picture of the lives of adults.

- Society could push toward crime at an early age!

- Life coerces us to do things we might not want.

- Adults Are More Vicious Than Children, Even If It Is a Cultured and Elegant Lady.

- Children have dignity.

- The real failure is the fear of failure.

- Don't stand still like a statue, and don't dread the might of ghosts.

- Winning his son and losing people's words was better than winning people's words and losing his son.

- So be brave and withdraw at the right time!

- He might be more concerned with his car insurance than his car, and he might fear for the life insurance more than for his life!

- Companies whose fuel is blood; they profit billions and zillions by igniting wars and inciting between nations and peoples. They intervene with the excuse of bringing peace but in reality, they intervene to prolong the war and stoke its lit wick; wherever they intervene, notice how the issues have become complicated and violence widespread and reconciliation a complete impossibility.

- And you'll find those who defend spilling the blood of innocents and cutting their limbs with the excuse of unavoidable necessity, to save humanity from an imminent danger or gloomy fate or terrorism about to happen… and how ugly humans are when they obliterate thousands of innocents then tweet from the electronic above apologizing for wasting lives by mistake.

- There is nothing like a painful experience.

- You've shortchanged yourself before they shortchanged you.

- A coward does not give themselves any worth or weight, and this is what makes them susceptible to exploitation and an easy meal for the greedy; no one can ride you unless you bow your back and show your need and weakness.

- At home I was used to looking for my old coat and finding my lost hat. I imagined life to be like this as well; you look for something like a job vacancy and find a surprise, but I never pictured that the surprise would be a landmine of racism that would explode in my face in this way.

- The hero does not die at the beginning of the film.

- My father hid a hurtful truth from me.

- Because I don't want you to suffer as I have suffered.

- We can change the world.

- The hero does not give up!

- Despite the political, military, and religious complications… nothing is impossible.

- After hardship there is only succor.

- Fear left me and I became the master of myself and owner of my fate.

- The job was no longer my lifeline, even though it had come at a time of great need and replacing it seemed near impossible, because there's an alternative to everything.

- I discovered my skills and the need my job had for

my abilities, which I had not noticed before.

- I knew well my self-worth, and I became able to negotiate and lay conditions, and I broke the one-sided equation.

- I respected myself and valued it, so I imposed my respect and value on them.

- I freed myself from my slavery to my job and work, and the job no longer owned me!

- I freed myself from the fear that had chained my thoughts and made me fall into a delusional captivity.

- I learned leaving my job was no longer a disaster nor the end of the world.

- I became certain that change only needs courage to overcome the fear of turning on the light switch.

- It was proven to me that showing your weakness and need will make people shortchange you and take advantage of you.

- Life had taught me lessons through a stunning disaster; it led it to me so I could wake up from my heedlessness and to free me from the captivity of the job.

- The skill of expecting the worst and the best: Why should you undertake a deal whose profit in the best of cases is meager? Or draw back from a deal which in its worst cases will not lose?

- The sudden imbalance could make you lose confidence in yourself and your skills and in others; loss of confidence is a destructive blight which hinders chances that heal you from an emotional, professional, domestic, or financial crisis.

- Don't believe that the university student differs too much from the children you knew in your youth; you will discover this from the first day. Prepare yourself for the worst; you will find in it the bitter and the sweet, and the lazy and the diligent.

- You will find university students who are not less than children in hooliganism; they call you a grind or "*harshan*" in Hebrew as if it were an insult, with the goal of detracting from your person and injuring your determination and diligence, out of envy; they don't want you to excel and study while they are playing.

- Then, life had in its way brought me together with university hooligans at a very early age, and what's strange is that it chose to pass these lessons on to my cheeks in my first year in school with the males, and it repeated them for me in my second year with the females, but I did not comprehend the lesson despite its tough applications and sexual variation.

- Some students depend on their mother and father like the Israelites depended on the Lord. And they might think that life is coincidence and luck.

- A tactical retreat is a profit not a flight!

- Today, commercial companies and work bosses and even the owners of sports clubs no longer suffice themselves with your curriculum vitae and technical skills.

- And today, the process of collecting data is considered the sole source of income for some companies specializing in this startling skill.

- Your electronic biography will determine your future without you being aware or meaning to. The world is being pushed toward this canyon; it is more truthful and more dangerous than any biography that you compose to send to a party courting their affection, and you must take warning and warn those around you from its danger on our future and the future of our works and projects. You don't know who is looking at your data now and drawing your picture for the intended circles; use the weapon of ciphers to your advantage.

- Oh, if only I had read my life book before entering university.

- There are no gaps in life and no stillness, because if you don't fill the gap someone else will fill it, and if you don't move on life's board to wherever you choose for yourself, some scoundrel will move you to wherever they choose for you.

- Solitude is not the worst choice.

- Know when to withdraw.

- When you have a financial and investment strategy that differs from your partner's vision, then the partnership cannot continue, even if you were the best friend in the world, and if it continues it will be unwillingly, like the partnership of two contentious spouses, neither the children nor the neighbors sleeping except to the din of their constant shouting.

- Incorrect logic is ingenious at putting down rebellions: All the red lights were blinking in warning, but the incorrect logic that I gained through the profits realized by blind deals before it made me confident in the success of this deal as well.

- She did not strike me physically, but my mother struck me with the cipher of shame, and so that was the first and last theft in my life.

- The book's idea made me get rid of complexes that prevented me, and logics that paralyzed me from moving and thinking in the correct direction that would serve my goals. I can say that the book produced itself by itself.

"THE ROD AND THE NET"

Here I've given you a magic rod, rather an extraordinary fishing net, and guided you on how to catch the impossible with it and imprison it within your hands. No barrier or impediment will stand in your way after today; you are from today onward the master of yourself, your fate in your hand. You've just been freed from the grip of the false idol that held you prisoner with the sorcery of its cowardly spells and frightened you with the ramming horns of delusion.

"YOUR NEXT STEP"

To make yourself available to read the next book, written by and starring you. Read it in its smallest details; correct the wrong logics that you have left to lead your steps to where you did not intend; take the reins of the logic of leadership and direct it to wherever you want; free yourself from your imprisoning logic.

Destroy the horns of your worshipped god, pull him down from the throne of his kingdom, and roar at the top of your voice announcing: I am the knight, and I am the king!

ABOUT THE AUTHOR

Rami Anabusi is a CPA and Economist born in 1976. He is a founding partner at the Accounting & Consulting firm KAA.

Uncensored exciting details of his real life adventures and business experiences are used attractively as examples throughout this book, from rebellion and bullying from both classmates and teachers, to embarrassments and lessons learned.

Rami attended the prestigious Hebrew University of Jerusalem between 1995-1999. He almost lost his life on his first visit to the university, and graduated successfully from the Faculty of Accounting and Economics.

As an Arab student in a predominantly Jewish population, he faced ill treatment and racism, experiences from which he draws valuable life lessons and which he boldly, honestly and freely shares across the four acts of this book. After many rejections from accounting firms across Jerusalem for the mandatory internship required for the CPA license, he finally found the work he most desired while preparing for his final exams — a job he found the courage to leave!